Landscape of Cybersecurity Threats and Forensic Inquiry

Joseph O. Esin

authorHOUSE®

AuthorHouse™
1663 Liberty Drive
Bloomington, IN 47403
www.authorhouse.com
Phone: 1 (800) 839-8640

Published by AuthorHouse 03/01/2018

ISBN: 978-1-5462-1705-3 (sc)
ISBN: 978-1-5462-1704-6 (e)

Print information available on the last page.

Any people depicted in stock imagery provided by Thinkstock are models, and such images are being used for illustrative purposes only. Certain stock imagery © Thinkstock.

This book is printed on acid-free paper.

Estimated Net Losses Due to Cybersecurity Attacks on Global Population

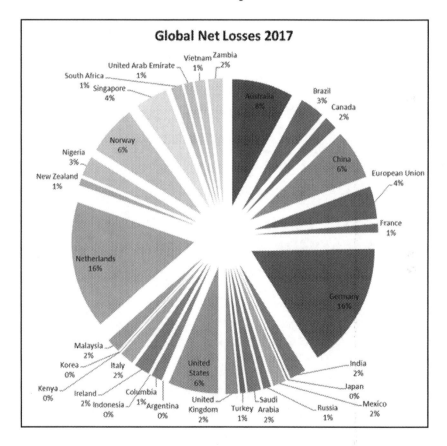

Contents

INTRODUCTION

An Author often pronounce proprietorship in the final product and I could not have done it alone. I have pursued during my life: fisherman, state land inspector, pastoral ministry, management information technology, hardware and software consulting, computer network installation, configuration and management, computer information instruction, research and writing. To be a researcher and writer was one of my first aspirations. It is true way back when I scrawled with my first article in Saint Francis Xavier Church bulletin, not perfectly written, but it was good, and I never gave up my dream. This book is the culmination of two distinct, but intertwine all-embracing support form Professor Emmanuel N. Ngwang; principal reviewer and Ms. Cynthia Wolfe, lead member of Author house editorial. The book begins by presenting strategies for the collection and analysis of computer forensic data and computer-related investigations. The book discusses significant advances in computer forensic, information technology server security domain, Institution of health insurance portability and Accountability Act (HIPAA), cloud computing technology and fundamentals of cryptography.

Computer forensics is a branch of digital forensic science relating to evidence found in computers, digital storage media such as internal hard drive, flash memory card, flash memory card reader, and USB flash drive. Computer Forensics emerged in the mid-1940s, and the rapid expansion of this technology is overshadowing by various computer transgressions and forensic inquiry. The emergence of personal computers, desktop computers, laptop computers, and tablets computers in 1970 with direct connective capability from anywhere and everywhere, has exposed law enforcement agencies to ongoing explosive encounters with cybercriminals. Domain is the strongest and weakest link in network history often compounded with the organization's inadequate information technology policy and training employees to protect system domain to battle cybercrime, cybersecurity threats and malicious attacks and unauthorized access into the network system. The book discusses the importance of Health Insurance Portability and Accountability Act, (HIPAA), enacted by the United States Congress and signed to law by President William J. Clinton in August 1996. The primary objective of HIPAA is to ensure individuals and employees opportunity to migrate from one healthcare plan to another will have continuity of coverage and will not be deprived of coverage under preexisting conditions. It strengthens the federal government's fraud enforcement authority in various states and regions. Cyber security professionals are not law enforcement officers, medical officers nor government agents. Cybersecurity officers are required to acquire thorough understanding of the impact of law relative to security operations.

Cloud technology provides security defense to the healthcare industry where organizations' network systems are monitored and maintained by a third-party provider and most of healthcare organizations are resisting adopting cloud technology as solutions that must include compliance to cloud service provider regulations which are reliable, scalable, affordable and meet regulatory requirements. Cryptography is derived from the Greek *KRYPTOS,* meaning hidden. The origin of cryptography is usually dated from about 2000 BC, with the Egyptian practice of hieroglyphics and consisted of complex pictograms with the full meaning known to few elite. The first known use of a modern cipher was by Julius Caesar (100 BC to 44 BC), who did not trust his messengers when communicating with his governors and officers and for this reason, he created a system in which each character in his messages was replaced by a character three positions ahead of it in the Roman alphabet. In recent times, cryptography has turned into a battleground of some of the world's best mathematicians and computer scientists with ability to securely store and transfer sensitive information. Most of this hiding was particularly important and necessary during the Cold War era and in today's cyber warfare when the slightest information can determine the fate of the world.

DISTINGUISHING GUIDES

Landscape of Cyber-Security and Forensic Inquiry provides an informational, step-by-step approach designed to empower professors, instructors, learners, cybersecurity professionals, IT directors and consultants on how to combat perpetrators of cybercrimes. Cyber-attacks on private and public organizations is growing exponentially and almost overpowering law enforcement agencies. Over the past few decades, cyber-attacks on global organizations have grown swiftly. Perpetrators of cyber-attacks have expanded their sophisticated strategies to include various facilities; hacking and cracking into private and public financial data and information. They have been involved in cyberwarfare, ransomware and malware that is currently affecting the global community. Cyber-attacks are currently threatening the global data and information transmission and communication landscape. International communities have intensified their complete dependency on technology, emails, and Internet for data and information transmission and communication. Our private and public transmission and communication systems are unrestricted and with no boundaries; the integration of mobile technology, electronic communication has increased their vulnerability and hosted more cyber-attacks, cybercrimes and perpetrators have become increasingly more sophisticated, organized and often fully aware of intended facilities. It is a given that local, state and federal government are responsible for their vulnerable citizens. In accordance with President John F. Kennedy's famous assertion, "Think not to what your country can do for you. think of what you can do for your country." Reinforcing President Kennedy's pronouncement relative to emerging open-ended, anytime and anywhere cyber-attacks; while governments are responsible for protecting their citizens, it is now imperative that citizens of the world community get deeply involved in protecting and securing the nations. The book *Landscape of Cyber-Security and Forensic Inquiry* provides solid foundation in various capacities; understating the nature of threats, steps that must be taken to mitigate vulnerabilities to protect against cyber security attacks.

Author's Comment

I am totally committed to listening and paying close attention to adopters—the professors, instructors, allied educators, information technology (IT) administrators, network consultants, and readers who adopt and use *Landscape of Cyber-Security and Forensic Inquiry* — international communities have intensified its complete dependency on technology, emails, and Internet for data and information transmission and communication. Our private and public transmission and communication systems are unrestricted and with no boundaries; the integration of mobile technology, electronic communication has increased and hosted more cyber-attacks, cybercrimes and perpetrators are sophisticated, organized and often fully aware of intended facilities.to formulate creative solutions to meet the needs of the current and future generations. And I fervently encourage active participation from readers in providing constructive suggestions and accurate information. Cogent input and useful, productive feedback will be deeply appreciated.

STRUCTURE OF THE BOOK

This book devotes each chapter to instruction, learning and professional certifications. Topics covered in each chapter are enumerated through the entire text including anthology of cybercrime, information technology server domain security institution of health insurance portability and accountability act, cloud computing security and evolution of cryptography. Over the past twenty-five years (25) years, cybersecurity has evolved from an opaque discipline often, enthroned into restricted facilities such as government agencies, financial institutions and military operations. Today, cybersecurity crusades constitute the mainstream operations in most private and public organizations across the globe. Contributing factors to national and international wide-spread of cybersecurity operations include unrestricted growth of the Internet, omnipresent connectivity, around-the-clock migration of vital data and information and intellectual property into digital format, rapid outsourcing of critical data and information to cloud provider. The new generation has witnessed the explosion of most strictly controlled regulations and laws such as Sarbanes Oxley (SOX), Health Insurance Portability and Accountability Act (HIPAA), Health Information Technology for Economic and Clinical Health Act (HITECH) US Department of Health and Human Services (HHS), Centers for Medicare and Medicaid Services (CMS), Assigned to the Office of Civil Rights (OCR), Medicare, Medicaid and State (CMS), State Children's Health Insurance Program (SCHIP), Designated Standards Maintenance Organization (DSMO), Workgroup for Electronic Data Interchange (WEDI). Washington Publishing Company (WPC), National Committee on Vital and Health Statistics (NCVHS), National Council for Prescription Drug Programs (CPDP). Family Education Rights and

Privacy Act (FERPA), and Children's Online Privacy Protection Act (COPPA)

The emergence of cybersecurity and parallel cybercrimes have decrypted into huge demand for skilled, experience training of cybersecurity professionals that I am sure will help to decrease the terrifying and mutating threats of cybersecurity across the globe. The world community, private and public organizations, needs cybersecurity professionals with real-world experience. This book provides an excellent and practical application of information systems and cybersecurity to protect against cyberbarriers and protectors. It is worth indicating that the continued cybersecurity threat is inevitable and must be confronted as global danger against human civilization. Due to unpredictive nature of cyber-attacks, the projected confrontation must begin through professional cybersecurity education, dedication and commitment. This book is written to provide a sturdy foundation to protect private and public organizations against unescapable cyber-attacks and steps to mitigate the dangers of unexpected vulnerabilities. The above operations have presented more complex and challenging threats to the landscape of the vulnerable global security.

Author's Background

Professor Joseph O. Esin, chief publishing editor of *The Journal of Educational Research and Technology (JERT)*, holds a Bachelor's of Science in Biology from Saint Louis University, Saint Louis, Missouri; a Master's of Arts in Religious Studies, with emphasis on Moral Theology, from the Society of Jesus College of Divinity, Saint Louis, Missouri; and a Doctorate in Computer Education and Technology from the United States International University, San Diego, California. The State of California awarded him a Lifetime Collegiate Instructor's Credential in 1989, and in 1996, the United States Department of Justice approved and conferred on him the honor of "Outstanding Professor of Research" in recognition of his contributions to academic excellence.

He met the selection criteria for inclusion in the 1992–93, 1994–95, 1996–97 and 2015–2016 editions of *Who's Who in American Education* for demonstration of achievement and outstanding academic leadership in computer information technology, thereby contributing significantly to the betterment of contemporary society. Furthermore, he met the selection criteria for inclusion in the 1993–94 edition of the *Directory of International Biography*, Cambridge, England, for his distinguished professional service in information technology. From 1988 to 2000, he served as a professor of computer information technology, and from 1991 to 2000, a director of higher education accreditation operations, in accordance with the guidelines set forth by the Commission on Colleges. He was appointed an associate dean of academic affairs and a deputy provost at Paul Quinn College, Dallas, Texas, from 1997 to 2000. He is currently a professor of computer information systems at Jarvis Christian College (JCC), Hawkins, Texas, where his peers just elected him Vice President of JCC 2017-2018 Faculty Governance. In addition, he is a visiting professor of research at.

the University at Calabar, Nigeria; and a research associate at the Botanical Research Institute of Texas (BRIT).

Professor Esin has published several articles in professional journals among which are "High Level of Teachers' Apprehension (HLTA): About the Use of Computers in the Educational Process" in the *Journal of Educational Media & Library Science* (*JEMLS*) in 1991; "Computer Literacy for Teachers: The Role of Computer Technology in the Educational Process," also in *JEMLS* (1992); "Faculty Development: Effective Use of Applications Software in the Classroom for Instruction" (*JEMLS*, 1993); "Strategies for Developing and Implementing Academic Computing in Colleges and Universities" (*JEMLS*, 1994); "Strategic Planning for Computer Integration in Higher Education through the Year 2000" (*JEMLS*, 1994); "The Challenge of Networking Technologies" (*JEMLS*, 1995); and "The Design and Use of Instructional Technology in Schools, Colleges and Universities" (*JEMLS*, 1997). He also published "Decay of the Nigerian Education System," in the *Journal of Educational Research and Technology* (*JERT*) in 2013; "The Emerging Impact of Information Technology on Education and the Community" (*JERT*, 2013); "Balanced Salary Structure for Academic Professors and Allied Educators as a Pathway to Quality Education" (*JERT*, 2014); and "The Discovery of Computer Information Technology as an Avenue for Educational Transformation in a Changing Society of Today and Tomorrow" in *International Organization of Scientific Research Journal of Engineering* (*IOSR-JEN*) in 2014. In 2016, he published "Overview of Cyber Security: Endangerment of Cybercrime on Vulnerable Innocent Global Citizens" in *The International Journal of Engineering and Science (IJES-2016)* and "Analog to Digital: Overcoming Widespread Implementation of Wireless Information Technology on a Vulnerable Global Society" (*JERT,2016*), Cybersecurity Professional Education and Inquiry (2017) in the *Washington Center for Cybersecurity Research and Development* (*WCCRD*-2017), Imminent Cybersecurity Threats and Vulnerability of Organizations and Educational Systems (*WCCRD*-2017), Escalating Outcome of Cyber-Attacks on Healthcare Organizations (WCCRD-2017) and Escalating Outcome of Cyber-Attacks on Healthcare Organizations (WCCRD-2017).

He served as a member of Doctoral Dissertation Committees at Southern Methodist University, Dallas, Texas (1998–2000); Jackson State

University, Jackson, Mississippi (2010–2011); and University of Calabar, Nigeria (2014–2015). He is the author of *The Power of Endurance* (2008), *The Evolution of Instructional Technology* (2011), *The Messianic View of the Kingdom of God* (2011), *Global Education Reform* (2013) and *System Overview of Cyber-Technology in a Digitally Connected Global Society* (2017). Professor Esin's current research emphasis is on the *Landscape of Cybersecurity Threats and Forensic Inquiry.*

He is guided by the philosophy that
"To achieve what is possible, you must attempt the impossible."

INDUSTRY EXPERT REVIEWERS

Dr. Emmanuel N. Ngwang
Professor of English and World Literature and Director of Quality
Enhancement Plan, Texas College, Tyler, Texas, USA.

CHAPTER 1

Anthology of Cybercrime

Computer Forensics (CF) is a branch of digital forensic science relating to evidence found in computers, digital storage media such as Internal hard drive, flash memory card, flash memory card reader, and USB flash drive. The primary goal of computer forensics is to examine digital media in forensically sound techniques with the aim of identifying, preserving, recovering, analyzing and presenting facts and opinions about the digital information to the public upon request. Computer Forensics emerged in the mid-1940s, and the rapid expansion of this technology was overshadowed by various computer transgressions and crimes. Computer crime is broadly understood as criminal acts in which a computer is the object of the offence and compatible tools all-inclusive cybercrimes. Per Bem, Feld, Huebner, Bem, (2008) studies on computer forensic, the first prosecuted case of computer crime was recorded in Texas, USA in 1966 and the indictment process resulted in a five-year sentence. In the 1970s, 1980s, 1990s and 2000s, personal computers, desktop computers, laptop computers, and tablets were found at home, offices, organizations, government agencies and everywhere. Today, law enforcement agencies are witnessing the emergence of new categories of crime re-classified as cybercrimes. As Esin (2017) noted, computer forensics is a structured discipline designed for investigation, using analysis techniques to gather and preserve evidence from a computing device for presentation in a court of law. The objective of computer forensics is to perform a structured investigation while maintaining a documented chain of evidence to find out exactly what happened on a computing device and who was responsible for any illegal operations.

Cybercrimes are new self-regulating computer crimes requiring reliable and trustworthy evidence to enhance successful prosecutions of the perpetrators. As Shinder and Tittle (2002) and Cross (2008) assert, computer forensics was designed to resolve, document and empower prosecution of computer crime to compile and present comprehensive and acceptable report in the court of law. Prior to 1980s, 1990s, and 2000s, most law enforcement agencies in every technologically advanced country became aware of cybercrimes, and had well-conceived laws and organizations such as Patriates Acts (PA) and Homeland Security respectively in place for investigation and prosecution of perpetrators of cybercrimes. Scientific research centers were established in most countries to battle cybercrimes and hardware and software manufacturers responded positively by producing various specialized tools to help in investigating culprits of cybercriminals. Per Bem, Feld, Huebner, Bem, (2008) and Jones, Bejtlich and Rose (2006), emergence of technological advancement is sponsoring large dimensions of cybercrimes, notably, most cybercrimes are often unreported and subsequently never prosecuted. In the United States, the annual Computer Crime and Security Surveys conducted by the Crime Scene Investigation (CSI) and Federal Bureau of Investigation (CSI/FBI) in 2006 show that from 1999 to 2006, 30% to 45% cybercrime, computer intrusion, mainly for fear of negative publicity were not reported. In Australia, the (AusCERT) surveys of 2006, indicated higher levels of 69% of law enforcement agencies respondents chose not to report incidence to any external party to avoid exposing lack of skills of respondents, and notably, 55% of cybercrimes cases were not reported (Bennett, 2011). It is not clear how most individuals expressed lack of confidence in law enforcement agency's capability, but unable to recognize remarkable increase in culprit's tactics to undermine law enforcement capability reporting and response to incidence. Per Shinder, (2002) and Brown (2015), the Locard exchange principle (LEP), known as Locard's theory, postulated by 20th Century forensic scientist Edmond Locard, is often applied to crime scenes where perpetrators of a crime arrive at the scene, bring something into the scene, leave something at the scene and where all contacts are noticeable. The LEP techniques involve objects perpetrators touches, unconsciously leaves behind such as fingerprints, footprints, hair, fibers, clothes, tool mark, scratches, blood and semen deposits or collects that can be used to bear mute witness against in the process investigation, response and reports to be presented in court.

Computer Forensics is a branch of digital scientific discipline relating to evidence found in computers and digital storage media. Bem, Feld, Francine, Huebner and Bem (2008) posited that computer forensics (CF) is the use of a wide-range of digital apparatus to examine to identify, preserve, recover, analyze, and present the facts and enlighten decisions and acceptable digitally oriented evidence. CF upholds awareness and knowledge, competency, **st**rategic data and information located on computer networking security centers. CF skills and expertise is imperative for network administrators, information technology directors, ddesigned to control various method of data recovery, analysis of latent evidence ranging from physiological and behavioral characteristic fingerprints, a hand, a face, an iris, personal traits, DNA evidence recovered from blood stains to the files on a computer hard drive (Garrain, 2017 & Esin 2017). Notably, CF is an exclusively new discipline that is attracted to most organizations such as higher education institution, civil organizations, government agencies, state and federal court systems amid existing limited standardization and consistency across the courts and cybersecurity industry.

CF trainings is a credible breakthrough in higher education enterprise. Most higher education administrators, chief executive officers and government officials tend to allocate limited portion of annual budgets to information technology, computer hardware, software and network security operations. As McClarkin, (2014) and Garrain, (2017) noted, data from International Data Corporation (IDC) recounted that the market for intrusion-detection and vulnerability-assessment software will reach 1.45 billion dollars in 2006 and report further highlighted that most organizations are deploying network security device systems such as intrusion detection systems (IDS), firewalls and proxies in growing numbers. As a result, CF relating crimes involving a computer often range across the spectrum of criminal activity, from child pornography to theft of personal data to destruction of intellectual property. Perchance, data, information, folders and files may have been deleted, damaged, and encrypted, CF examiner and investigator must be familiar with an array of methods and software to prevent further damage in the recovery process. Persistent data are often stored on a local hard drive, separate medium and preserved when the computer system is turned off. Volatile data is stored in a memory, or exist in transit and may be lost when the computer loses power and is turned off. Furthermore, volatile data is ephemeral, resides in registries, cache, and random-access memory (RAM) and requires experienced examiner and investigator to identify means to recover the items. System administrators and security personnel must be educated with skills and understanding of how routine computer auditing and network administrative tasks can affect the forensic process, the potential admissibility of evidence in court and the subsequent ability to recover data that may be critical to the identification and analysis of a security incident (Casey, 2010).

Cybersecurity Literacy

Cyber security literatures, writings and books tend to focus on complex digital network systems and protection of private and public organizations and little consideration is directed to providing users with training, expertise and technical skills needed to defend organizations' network systems. As Esin (2017) and Assenter and Tobey (2011) maintain, government agencies, higher education institutions and organizations must press forward to establish a well-structured cyber literate professional development training (CLPDT) program to provide users with computer knowledge and technical expertise to handle continued cybersecurity The objective of CLPDT guidelines must include cybersecurity skills needed by employees to preempt cyber-attack, avoid conspiring with co-workers and outsiders, to prohibit unauthorized access to the organization's confidential and restricted information on network systems. Most employees have limited backgrounds and are somewhat intimidated to operate computer hardware, operating systems, vertical and integrated applications programs that often tend to slow down productivity. It is a thought-provoking process for private and public organizations to implement cybersecurity system and overlook the importance of CLPDT. Continued implementation of CLPDT is an important instrument of productivity and advancement for private and public organizations and is an unavoidable requirement to prepare users for skills and expertise to overcome cybersecurity literacy including the use of wired and wireless technologies and access to the Internet (LeClair, 2016 & Givens, 2015). Software ooperating system program is designed to manage computer hardware, software resources and system services; therefore, users must acquire fundamental backgrounds on operating systems, application programs, configurations, security settings, built-in utilities, file storage structure, ability to help in minimizing the likelihoods of executing redundant commands, and interfering with network operations. As Esin (2016), LeClair (2016); Fitzgerald and Schneider (2015) Esin (2016) noted, program outlines for (CTPDT) must include the user's skills and expertise on the following:

1. Activating and deactivating most application programs, system utilities, check network status to conform to the existence of valid Internet Protocol (IP) address, subnet mask, default gateway, run most computer network commands such as ping, ipconfig, net config, and net user to examine network connectivity. Such expertise includes the ability to install, configure and troubleshoot network systems, organize and monitor software update mechanism validating if the computer operating system is accepting security patches and system applications updates;

2. Executing distinct categories of backups operations including Full **Back up** techniques used to backup files and folders selected for backup. Subsequent backups will include entire list of files and will be backed up again. The process is fast and easy as the complete list of files are stored each time it is done. However, the process is time consuming and takes up a lot of storage space compared to incremental and differential backups. **Incremental backup** includes changes made since the last backup; it is faster than full backup and storage space used is less than a full backup and much less than differential backups. In this process, the restoration space is slower than full backup and a differential backup. **Differential backup** includes all changes made since the last full backup and the response rate is faster than a full backup. The storage space used is less than a full backup, but somewhat more than incremental

backups; this restoration ability is slower than full backup and faster than incremental backups. **Mirror Backup** are mirrors of the source being backed up. Deleting source files will ultimately delete mirror backups files. This could be by human accident and/ or virus assault **Full Computer Backup is when** individual's files, images of the hard drives, work documents, picture, videos and audio files system files, registry, programs, hard drives, hardware drives emails are backed up, and data files can be restored exactly as were backed up. **Local backup** protects digital content from hard drive failures, virus attacks, accidently deleting data files, and stored in proximities, such as office, building, external hard drive, compact disk (CD) and network attached storage (NAS). **Offsite Backup is used by o**rganizations to store backup media, cartridges, financial institution's safe deposit box, and where external storage media are stored in different geographic locations from computer central command. Offsite backup provides extra protection against cyber-theft, fire, floods, tornado, hurricane and natural disasters. **Online Backup** Ongoing backup medium connected to sources located offsite through the Internet and network system with limited human intervention and storage data centers are often located away from the network operation center and **Cloud Backup is** used interchangeably with online backup and remote backup connected over the Internet and involves authorized login credentials.

3. Understanding weighty differences relating to encrypting data files located on a partition, and encrypting files on entire network to protect data files, restricted information against unauthorized access. Users must be aware of categories of cable networking devices and components including routers, bridges, repeaters, firewalls and intrusion detection systems, wired and wireless network benchmarks, Wi-Fi, Bluetooth, Smartphones, wireless access points, cinderblock walls in the building that are often used to exfiltrate confidential information and stir users to believing they are using valid network and leaving confidential information vulnerable to cybercriminals.

4. The pilgrimage on becoming cyber-literate required local area network (LAN) and wide area network(WAN) users to be equipped with guiles and expertise to battle perpetrators of cyber threats, and employees who can be reliable sources of mischief, enticing threats from outsiders. Per Esin (2017) and LeClair, (2016), current employees have official permission and privileges to resources in organization network systems; however, recluses remain dominant sources of threats to organizations. Cyber threats emerge in different setups and CTPD must pay greater attention to the malware programs. Indeed, a malware program is analogous to various types of hostile and intrusive programs such as computer viruses, worms, Trojan horses, ransomware, spyware, adware, scareware, and other malicious programs. Malware is stealthy software designed to steal information on private and public computers for an extended period without users' knowledge. Malicious software is used to disrupt computer operations, gather sensitive information, gain access to an individual's and/or an organization's computer network systems, and display unsolicited and annoying advertising. It can deliberately alter system network operations relating to unintentional harm due to some deficiency. Users must be equipped with expertise to identify malware delivery techniques including unsolicited emails, tough to delete rootkits, social engineering, and phishing scams phone calls. The substitute name for cybersecurity literacy is information security literacy and data security literacy which operates on limited technical skills required to protect organizations against hackers, cybercriminals, crackers, and cyberterrorists. CTPD must be entrenched with effective pedagogy and not in fundamentally half-finished top-twenty bullet point list of security activities. Indeed, CTPDT is a prime key to combat intrinsic threats to data information literacy. Private and public organizations are swamped with screen pop-ups warning users about patch updates, antivirus signatures, firewall exceptions, suspicious emails, and malware threats with narrow professional expertise on cyber security education.

5. Implementing CTPDT is a pedagogical approach to provide users with context, firsthand skills to be proactive in applying cybersecurity best practices when confronted with a novel situation and cybersecurity threats. On February 17, 2016, in the wake of San Bernardino incidence, the United States magistrate judge in California ordered Apple to comply with the Federal Bureau of Investigation's (FBI) request to assist in bypassing the passcode lock of the San Bernardino gunman's iPhone. Hours later Apple published an open letter by Tim Cook explaining that creating a tool to bypass this specific iPhone would jeopardize the security of all iPhones. The battle between personal privacy and information gathering relating to Apple and security measures has been going on for quite a while and the government continues to face challenges on matters relating to specific iPhone used by a terrorist during San Bernardino in the United States. Apple executives faced up to FBI's court order, challenged the White House for supporting the department of justice indication that Apple's resistance will create credible avenue for more terrorist attacks on American soil. The FBI needed direct access to text messages, notes, photos, emails, and data saved on the suspected terrorist's iPhone to preserve critical data to assist in investigation. To be sure, the government wants to protect the vulnerable innocent citizens and Apple wants to protect their customers-based. However, the FBI posited that data protected behind the terrorist's iPhone passcode could offer critical evidence leading to San Bernardino's plan and execution of attacks. The government, FBI and Apple corporation operate on different rates of recurrence of cybersecurity.

Cybercrime Investigations

Computer Forensics Criminal Investigations (CFCI) is actively in progress and will continue to be indispensable to search, arrest and convict criminals, terrorists, sexual predators, and murderers off the streets. Digital evidences are legally admissible in court of justice. Per Bennett (2011) the none existing legal boundaries on the use of the Internet across the globe, cybercriminal's malicious intentions are growing more sophisticated and are on the threshold of challenging and preventing CFCI from reaching its full potential. Consequently, most cyber criminals, terrorists, sexual predators, murderers, to mention just a few often use mobile phone, the Internet and other electronic devices to recruit their criminal counterparts. In the process, most criminals fail to cover their tracks when using the Internet to execute criminal activities and completely ignore the fact that computer systems can retain data and files on system hard drive even when items are deleted, allowing CFCI to track criminal activities. Evidence from past and current criminal records indicate that culprits tend to delete incriminating files, folders, data and information from the system hard drive; regrettably, deleted items always remain in a binary format due to the residual representation of the confirmation file, folders, and data. Information deletion simply remains hiding from the user whereas, the original file is still stationary in the memory and can always be recovered (Tohid, 2012).

CFCI: Data Files in RAM

System folders, data, files and information are often overwritten and lost due to the volatile nature of memory and storage location in the memory. Random-access memory chip (RAMC) is designed to retrieve data from memory, help programs to function efficiently and validate that each time a computer is switched off, the RAM loses most of the data stored in the system. RAM is a volatile memory and folders, data, files and information preserved in a hard drive are in a persistent memory. RAM is constantly swapping rarely used folders, data, files and information on the hard drive to replace new data; thus, contents in the swap file can be overwritten and investigators often lose more evidence because computer files and data do not exist indefinitely and existing contents can be safely used by CFCI during crime investigation by detectives and may constitute law enforcement officers' crime analysis folders (Last, 2012).

CFCI: Global Position System

CFCI-Global Position System (GPS) software programs are embedded in smartphones and satellite navigation systems; codenamed Satnav, this software is designed to help CFCI in tracking the whereabouts of cybersecurity culprits, terrorists, sexual predators, and murderers to keep them off the street and protect innocent community. Manufacturers of software programs for computer forensics and satellite navigators are equipped with the tools and technology for GPS to acquire evidence that can be acceptable in the court of law. It is noted that the evidence that can be recovered from GPS software is limited due to a list of addresses. Per Last's (2012) assessment, modern current software does not record the time when the addresses were archived, whether the address was recorded by a person, automatically recorded, or user's intent for storing addresses was associated with crime investigation and response. Despite limitations, GPS evidence is crucial to the success of many prosecutions. As noted by Cashell, Jackson, Jickling and Webel (2014), four armed suspects accused of robbing a bank in the United Kingdom were convicted because each suspect owned a vehicle containing incriminating evidence, such as bank's address and addresses and crucial information of the other three suspects. As the Scottish National High-Tech Crime Unit continued searching and investigating GPS devices of vehicles that pass-by, thousands of addresses were uncovered; most of the addresses turned out with connections to crime scene. In 2011, U.S. forces successfully found the Pakistani compound where Osama bin Laden was located and killed by tracking satellite phone calls made by his bodyguards. Albeit, the fact that GPS evidence on its own may not be enough to establish a motive, GPS evidence often provides invaluable leads and convincing and admissible evidence in court (Tohid, 2012).

CFCI-Password Encryption

Cyber-criminals have grown and become vigilant in attempt to rawhide vital data and information all the way through encryption techniques. Spruill (2012) and Stallings (2015), in their studies on digital forensics and encryption noted that minority population of cyber-criminals operates on limited proficiency to implement encryption program on a continued-use basis and ability to encrypt data and files. Perpetrators of cyber-crimes are noted in their attempts to conceal vital data, information, folders and files for protection against law enforcement officer's investigation of the crime scene. Certainly, if most data, information, folders and files on a hard drive are encrypted, investigators can analyze unencrypted copies found elsewhere on the device to unearth data, files, folders and information. Computer users tend to reuse passwords, investigators can locate passwords very easily using a decipherable technique to gain access to protected files. Computer data, files, folders and documents are created with Microsoft Office - 2007, 2010 and modern 365 are often developed and configured to generate copies each time a document is modified to ensure the deleting documents are permanently removed from the memory. Notably, Microsoft software programs are entrenched with built-in and back-up strategies that pose very challenging and demanding tasks for cybercriminals to completely delete convicting court evidence.

CFCI-Mobile Devices

Law enforcement officers and cybercrime investigating teams' primary objective is to exploit computer system anomalies, obtain evidence and high-tech limitations that can often compromise the investigating process. The obtainable decorum designed to assist investigating teams in handling a mobile device found at a crime scene is to immediately power-off such mobile device. The prime reason to turn-off mobile device on the crime scene is to preserve the life of the battery and prevent an outside source from using the remote wipe features to interfere with the mobile phone's contents. As soon as the mobile phone is turned off, members of the investigating team are convinced that the device no longer accepts calls, text messages, emails and incoming and outgoing data that can overwrite the evidence currently stored in the system (Tohid, 2012 & Hoyte, 2012). The trivial effect of immediately turning off a mobile device at the crime scene often to theloss of vital data, and most downloaded files are likely to be corrupted.

CFCI-Solution

Proposition 1. The collaborative approach to minimize the looming CFCI operation must include the computer and mobile device manufacturers to develop in-built defense technology and to form alliances with service providers to monitor and shield connection to network systems. In-built defense devices, instruments, machines and tools will provide systematic conduit guiding investigating officials not to worry about turning-off the device on the crime scene. Per Tohid's (2012) assertion, the in-built radio frequency (RF) bag in iPhone tends to shield and keep signals from entering and leaving the device during an investigating process. Last (2012), in his studies on computer analysts, posited that errors in locating signals in the isolated crime scene range up to 300 meters and 95 percent of GPS measurements fall within 5 meters of the exact position. In non-isolated, large geographical and thick forest regions, solar weather and multistory building can disrupt and block satellite signals. Sophisticated cybercriminals know how to purposely use jammers to disrupt and block investigation officials' tracking systems.

Proposition 2. Collaborative approach to minimize the looming CFCI must involve the use of audit communications channels and monitoring systems in tracing cybercriminals. It is a popular perception that GPS related evidence are sketchy and not likely to convince the judge and the jury as sustainable court evidence. The audit communication channel will provide reliable recovering proof to circumvent skepticism from the judge or jury and decrease errors afflicting GPS data measurements. If not, the defense team can suppress the GPS evidence if data and records are significantly faulty and unreliable (Bennett, 2011, Tohid, 2012 & Reese, 2009).

Proposition 3. A collaborative approach to minimize the looming CFCI must involve keeping track of the growing cyber-technology devices. Advancement in cyber-technology equipment and devices and the sophistication of cybercriminals presents a benchmark for well-structured protective measures across the border. There is urgent need for professional training to obtain and preserve evidence, to acquire modern investigating devices and create and maintain partnership with International Criminal Police Organization (Interpol) to design and implement cybercrime stratagems for information exchange (Tohid, 2012; Reese, 2009).

Proposition 4. Another collaborative approach to minimize the looming CFCI must include the purchase of modern training equipment for forensic investigations implanted with in-built surveillance equipment, modern-day cyber-technology computers and cyber-mobile devices to protect investigating team against cybercriminals. Bennett (2011) proposed that the modern-day cyber-technologies must include electronic surveillance to monitor out-going and in-coming traffic, Internet surveillance to track suspicious activities in preparation for global safety.

Progressively, human populations everywhere and anywhere revolve around and depend on the use of cyber-technology and electronic devices regardless of geographical locations. Electronic surveillance is designed to keep law-abiding citizens safe. Today, public and private organizations such as financial, Banks, government facilities, and higher education institutions are increasingly depending on electronic devices to store and protect data facilities. Electronic surveillance in the Banks, homes organizations, government agencies and educational system is helping law enforcement officials and investigator teams in tracking cybercriminals much faster than in the past. Most programs such as *HLN Files, Investigation ID, American Most Wanted* (by John Wash) *and Forty-Eight (48) Hours* often reveal the importance of human surveillance through digital communication and telephone calls to investigators and police detective offices in helping to bring cybercriminals to justice.

Overview of Cybercrime

Cybercrime is intentional and illegal activities involving using a computer application, cultured and advanced than the past to gain, steal, and/or disrupt access to people's and companies' information and database. Cybercrimes are often categorized into two groupings; internal and external system attacks. Per Gerrain (2017), internal system attacks occur when there is a breach of trust from employees and cohorts within the organizations. Perpetrators of cybercrimes are mission-driven and often have specific objectives and purposes. They usually have authorized access to the organization's network system and are capable of planting malware, worm and Trojan horses in the system. The internal system attack is very difficult to identify because such attacks tend to affect all component in the organization's network system. Malware, worm and Trojan horses assault has the ability to affect, disorganize and possibly damage entire components of the organization's security, integrity and confidentiality embedded in the network system. Most information technology (IT) directors, network administrators and managers operate on the hypothesis that the network system is safe from internal and external attack by fortifying the network with firewalls and protecting measures. As Gerrain (2017) and Spruill (2012) reveals that internal assaults can cost individuals, organizations and higher education institutions millions of dollars because it is extremely difficult to identify which of the employees are snooping around the network for any reason. Most external assaults emerge as the result of none compliance with information security, policies or procedures set forth by the organization. Assailants are often disgruntled employees, individuals within the organization hired by the external entity to destroy a competitor's reputation for personal or political reasons.

Genesis of External Cyber-Assault

Most individuals involved in the process are believed to have been linked to cybersecurity operatives. In a sweeping set of announcements, the United States released samples of malware, indicators of Russian cyberactivity, and network addresses of computers frequently used by the Russians agents to launch attacks. Emergence of information super-highway, cyber-technology, cybersecurity, conventional internet connection, transmission and communication is shoving Democratic National Committee (DNC), Republican National Committee (RNC) and the global population closer to cyberwar. The world communities have never been exposed to the threats of cyber-security assault on democracy, local, state and national election until today and even if it did happen, such operatives were underestimated with minor impacts on the world population.

Battling External Cyber-Assault

Per Real Fly, December 10, 2016 11:51 p.m. "The Central Intelligent Agency (CIA) moves to invalidate United States Presidential Election by Blaming Russian Hacking." (2016). On December 9, 2016, Washington Post reported a secret CIA assessment concludes that the Russian government was trying to help the president-elect win the 2016 election and alluded to a leak from inside the CIA, saying they had a report that showed evidence that Russia hacked the elections to elect Donald Trump. Source such as Reuters The CIA has concluded that Russia intervened in the 2016 election to help President-elect Donald Trump win the White House, and not just to undermine confidence in the U.S. electoral system and lacking full understanding of the cyber-threat Moscow posed to the United States of America. As a result, the civil rights legend Representative. Mr. John Lewis, (D-GA.) and prominent Democrats in Congress vowed to skip Mr. Trump's inauguration, charging that Russian interference in the United States' 2016 national election delegitimizes Mr. Trump's presidency (*Associate Press*, Sunday, 15, January 2017). Cyber-assault involves the use of cyber-technology for connection, data and information transmission and communication in two major phases— wired and wireless operations. Wired connection is limited to physical cable layout and equipment, while wireless connection is unlimited involving human invisibility, challenges and security risks. On March 27, 2017 former vice-president of the United States, Mr. Dick Cheney, not willing to toe the party line, spoke in New Delhi at the Economic Times' Global Business Summit about Russia's criminal intents. He strongly disparaged Mr. V. Putin on his involvement in on-line subterfuge with the aim of defeating Hillary Clinton and installing Mr. Trump his puppet friend in the White House as an assault to the United States fundamental democratic processes. Per Kinyenje (2015), the landscape of proliferation of wireless technologies' wave of unlimited connection has created a credible bottleneck between cyber-assault and defense capabilities because public and private organizations, law enforcement units, crime investigation units, department of defense, department of transportation, aviation industry and cybercriminals use same cyberspace "one-way" connection, transmission and communication in all operations.

Quantifying Cybercrime

Cybercrime is the illegal exploitation of computer technologies, use of electronic devices and the Internet to commit crimes such as identity theft, information theft, embezzlement, hacking, cyberbullying, cyberstalking, and/or to cause damage to an organization's network system. According to Shinder (2002), cyber is not a component of criminal offense, but the means to commit crime and use of computer technology to provide new tactics to commit primordial crimes by the creation of premeditated and thought-out assault against vulnerable innocent global communities. Cybercrime has adopted a new name and look, related to criminal activities such as identity theft, computer theft, information theft, piracy, cyberterrorism, social engineering, cyber-espionage via spyware, child pornography, embezzlement, mismanagement of public funds, hacking, cyberbullying, cyberstalking as designated by the globally acceptable bilingual operative expression. IT directors, law enforcement officers, investigators, private detectives and judicial systems are unenthusiastic to discuss cybercrime activities in the public. The FBI, National Computer Crime Squad (NCCS), Federal Computer Fraud and Abuse Act (FCFAA) of 1986 are set forth to investigate cybercriminals cross multiple state, national and international boundaries. FBI, NCCS and FCFAA's range of investigations is extended to public switched telephone networks (PSTN), public and private organization's computer network intrusions, system integrity, software piracy, and cyber-espionage (Grama, 2016 & Johnson, 2011).

Most States in the continental United States have laws relating to regulating and enforcing of cybercrime by the state legislative branch and national governing constituent. Texas state's section of Penal Codes on Computer Crimes defines cybercrime as a Breach of Computer Security. Texas Penal Code Section 33.02 outlines cybercrime as expressive knowledge, gaining access to individuals and an organization's computer network without authorized consent. The penalty for violators is scaled per dollar amount lost by the victim and benefits to the offender. California Penal Code (Section 502) posted eight (8) acts that constitute cybercrime to include attempt to alter, damage, use of computer data to execute a scheme to defraud, deceive, export, wrongful earning of money, property, technology services without permission, disrupting of an organization's network services, assisting persons to unlawfully access a computer and introducing contaminant into the organization's network systems (Shinder and Tittel, 2002; Cross, 2008; & Eastton, 2011). It is worth indicating that attempts to protect innocent citizens against cybercrimes defer depending on the bye-laws, regulations and compliance within each state's national and international boundaries.

During the Vienna (2002) 10th United Nation Congress on the Prevention of Cybercrime and Treatment of Offenders (UNCPCTO) participants clearly attested that the global community is faced with unprecedented challenges posed by the modern-day, increasingly global cybercrime. This stand was a clear recognition that one nation by itself cannot cope successfully with the rapid growth of transnational cybercrime. Fighting cybercrime in its entirety is open-ended and unlimited because cybercrime agents are sophisticated and well-organized whereas, victims are vulnerable innocent individuals. Men, women, children and organizations continue to grieve in the hands of heartless criminals robbing them of their dignity, basic rights, possessions, health and lives. In the advent of globalized threats from organized cybercriminals, the united world community must step up to build new and better fences against cybercrime in all its forms and manifestations and to make sure that such criminals will not be allowed to go unpunished. Per UN (2000) regulations, the statute of cybercrime was designated into two components - computer cybercrime and computer-related cybercrime. Cybercrime is limited, relating to illegal conduct directed by means of electronic operations targeting the security of computer systems, data and information processed in the system. However, cyber-technology cybercrime is far-reaching relating to illegal activities committed by means of computer network, the Internet communication, unauthorized access and use, and distribution of prohibited information. The use of computer and the Internet for cybercrime is the highest growing physical crime in our generation today.

The world communities are more interconnected today than ever before. The advantages that accrue from this interconnectedness are counterbalanced, if not outweighed by the corresponding increase in the dangers related to risks of theft, credit card fraud, abuse, hacking, cracking, cyber-terrorism, cyberterrorism, financial fraud, cyber deformation, copyrights, password trafficking, telecommunication crime. Today, the citizens of the world kingdom are more vulnerable to cyber-assaults, security breaches, spam, spear phishing, electronic fraud, spyware, cybertrespass, cyber-espionage than in the past decades. Across the globe (in the United States, France, Belgium, Turkey, United Kingdom, Nigeria, to mention a few) we are witnessing law enforcement officers risking their lives to protect and defend the free global kingdom, working non-stop to investigate broad-range cybercrimes. Most of these criminals are apprehended, prosecuted and put in jail. Per terrorist attacks in New York City, Pennsylvania, and Washington, DC, on September 11, 2001, the United States Congress enacted the Patriot Act (PA) in 2001 and the Homeland Security Act in 2002. The Department of Homeland Security (DHS) is designed to support most federal government agencies in investigating high-profile and sophisticated criminals. All-inclusive objective of DHS is to disrupt and defeat cyber criminals by recruiting and training of technical experts, developing standardized methods, and to broadly share cyber information and response to protect citizens of free world. DHS teams are highly trained investigators on cybersecurity; they are experts, skilled in interrupting malicious cybercriminal's target and responding within reasonable time to save lives.

As Heintze and Thielborger, (2016) reported, the Cybercrime Prevention Act (CPA) of 2012, was officially chronicled as Philippines Republic Act (PRA) No. 10175 and approved as a law on September 12, 2012. PRA (2012:10175) is viewed as an old law set forth to protect cybersquatting, cybersex, child pornography, identity theft, an illegal access to data and information. The statute of PA (2001), PRA (2012), CPA (2012) and DHS (2001) defined identity theft and identity fraud as a crime that involves unlawfully access and using of public and private organizations' and individuals' data and information for economic benefits. It also includes the unauthorized use of access to and use of Social Security numbers, financial information, Bank accounts, debit and credit card numbers, telephones, and addresses by cybercriminal for personal profit at owner's expense (Grama, 2016; Heintze & Thielborger, 2016).

Canons of Computer Forensics and Response.

Cybercrime is often intended to trigger mental and physical pain, loss of property, pillory, loss of intellectual property, violation and infringement of security rights, and financial burden on vulnerable innocent citizens of this free global community (Aquiline, Casey & Malin, 2008). Perpetrators of cyber security attacks often operate on independent mindsets, on behalf of group of none-law abiding citizens. The perpetrators often have specific targets to hack into the systems, blog authorized user access, damage organization data and information, engage in illegal activities with the Internet to disrupt, install malicious programs, stalking Internet activities and creating identity theft. In response, computer inquiry experts work to relentlessly identify the source and preserve evidences, extract and document every process, validate and analyze evidences, formulate solutions and recommendations to prevent future occurrences. Operative inquiry and response must include reconnaissance, inquiry, research, documentation, analysis and preservation of evidence.

Forensic inquiry and response must be conducted by authorized, experienced and professionally skilled officials such as those produced by the Association of Chief Police Officers (ACPO, 2015) who have been drilled on rigors of the operational guiding principles of the response team. In 2015, ACPO established four guiding principles relating to computer-based electronic evidence and the four guiding principles must be adopted and executed in the latitude of computer forensic examination and response. Per Easton and Taylor (2011) and Givens (2016), the scope of inquiry and response must involve restriction of illegal exploitation of computer technologies, use of the Internet to commit cybercrimes such as identity theft, information theft, embezzlement, hacking, cyberbullying, cyberstalking, and damage to organizations' network systems. The global population needs cyber-technology advocates to guide and protect against new tactic of committing post-historic cybercrime using the Internet. In 2015, ACPO established four guiding principles relating to computer-based electronic evidence must be adopted and executed in all latitude of computer forensic Investigations:

- Data stored in a computer or storage media must not be altered or changed, as those data can be later presented in the court.

- Members of investigating team must be competent in handling the original data stored on a computer, device, and storage media as evidence and be willing to explain the relevance and course of their actions.

- An audit trail and relevant documentation of all processes applied to computer-based electronic evidence must be created and preserved. An independent third party should be able to examine those processes and achieve the same result.

- Members of investigating team must fully assume responsibility and be accountable to make sure that the law and the ACPO principles are adhered to during the process of investigation.

Computer Forensic-Files Systems- A computer is an electronic device and can be programmed to accept unprocessed data input, process data processing, store data Storage, generate processed information Output, transmit, communicate data and information into the system Communication (IPSOC).

Forensics – The literary meaning of forensics is "bring to the court." Forensics inquiry and response involves investigation, recovery and analysis of latent evidence. Hidden evidence often takes many forms, from fingerprints, scratches on doors, window to DNA evidence recovered from blood stains and files on a computer hard drive. Microsoft Windows servers - New Technology File System (NTFS) and Master File Table (MFT) contain data and files in a disk. The records in the MFT are metadata and files stored in MFT are classified into two groupings: resident and non-resident portions. A file of less than 512 bytes are resident files stored in MFT partition and files of more than 512 bytes are stored outside of MFT partition (Smith, 2008). Once a file is deleted from Windows NT directory, anticipated deleted files are automatically renamed by Network Operating System (NOS) and often moved to Recycle Bin with an assigned, unique identity.

Operating System (OS) stores data, files, folders and information on the path of an original file known as info2 file. Info2 often works directly with Recycle Bin and holds record of the original files, folders and paths with ability to restore these data from the trash. Upon emptying the Recycle Bin, data, files, folders and embedded in Infor2 get emptied as well. Info2 is designed for Microsoft Windows computer forensics and can be edited using free tools known as rifiuti2. After a file is deleted from the Recycle Bin, clusters are marked as available for new data. NTFS is often more efficient than Fat Allocated Tables (FAT) and NTFS is faster in reclaiming deleted space. NTFS disks are a data stream, and can be affixed into another existing file. Unlike NTFS, FAT is often created to keep track of the contents of a computer hard drive used by Microsoft Operating systems and table is a chart of numbers parallel to cluster addresses on a computer hard drive. **Forensics** is also an art of using technology for investigating, establishing, collecting and preserving data and facts as evidence in a court of law. Forensic is specifically application of science and technology designed to collect, preserve, and analyze logical evidence during an investigation. Most IT directors, managers and lead IT team must be cognizant of the legal implications of forensic activities and associated security policies, decisions, and technical actions that follow existing laws. Most forensic activities are carried out in a normal traditional format in specific laid-out steps to validate admissible evidence in court of law. Per Harris's (2016) assertion, experienced and skilled forensic teams must establish seven (7) goal oriented steps with emphasis toward accomplishing acceptable outcome. The projected result requisites must include identification, preservation, collection, examination and analysis of evidence gathered on the crime scene, and ultimately presentation and decision making based on the authentication of evidence in the court of law.

Child Exploitation and Obscenity Section (CEOS) was created in 1987 to protect the welfare of America's children and communities by enforcing federal criminal statutes relating to the exploitation of children and obscenity. The High Technology Investigative Unit (HTIU), created in 2002, authorizes experts to prosecute child exploitation cases and investigate high-technology child exploitation crimes (Johnathan, 2013; Smith, 2008). CEOS and HTIU are providing tremendous assistance to the Department of Justice in its continuous endeavors to enforce federal child exploitation laws and prevent the exploitation of children.

Per Smith (2008), CEOS and HTIU computer forensic team assigned to Criminal Division of the Department of Justice are providing advice and professional staff development training to federal prosecutors, law enforcement personnel and government officials, participating in national and international meetings on training, policy development and security operations including innovative solutions to ongoing cybersecurity threats. The High Technology Investigative Unit (HTIU), designed to conduct forensic analysis on computer evidence in federal cases and child exploitation crimes, is working diligently with federal agencies; the FBI, Homeland Security Investigations (HSI), and the Postal Inspection Service in prosecuting cybercriminals across the country. As Eastton and Taylor (2011) point out, HTIU often provides most accurate, up-to-date report on forensic inquiry and assist law enforcement agents in investigating and prosecuting cybercriminals. HTIU teams are often required to assist in child exploitation and craving internet, forensic research, development of investigative tools and techniques.

Forensic Toolkit (FTK)is one of the World's reliable Standard Digital Forensic Investigation Solution. FTK is an acceptable court-cited digital investigations platform designed to strengthen the speed, stability, durable of data and information and to provide comprehensive processing, forthright indexing, filtering, wide-searching and prompt analysis of evidence (Bejtlich & Rose, (2006). FTK architecture design emphasis is database-driven, enterprise-class structure to handle massive data sets, built-in data visualization, explicit image detection technology to rapidly discern, reporting, documentation, analysis of pertinent material during investigation. As NISTFTK Imager (2003) noted, interior and exterior operation with most Access Data's solutions often allows massive correlating of data access from various sources, such as, computer hard-drives, mobile devices, network data and Internet storage. FTK competency is designed as a leading digital investigation solution operation capable of lessening productive time and efforts through response and inquiry, allowing sufficient time interval to review data and identify relevant evidence, and finally assembling all in a single centralized location. FTK is entrenched in Cerberus capability. *"Cerberus is a monster in the shape of a three-headed dog guarding the entrance into* *the infernal regions and a vigilant custodian, guardian of a genus of East Indian serpents allied to the pythons. Cerberus or Kerberos in Greek and Roman mythology is a multi-headed dog"* (www.definitions.net/definition/ (Cerberus; McClarkin, 2014, Bennett, 2011; and NIST, 2003). FTK frequently identifies risky files capable of potentially contaminating the system while at the same time avoiding exporting such data. It empowers investigating teams with the ability to receive actionable intelligence while waiting for the malware investigators to perform deeper, more detail and time-consuming analysis to authenticate the evidence in the court of law.

Access Data's Password Recovery Toolkit (PRTK) is designed to assist in conducting forensic investigations utilizing Microsoft Windows systems. PRTK is an industry-led solution assisting in password recovery which utilizes many different environments to provide specific, password-cracking related functions. Per Jones, Bejtlich and Rose (2006), law enforcement agencies and corporate security professionals performing computer forensic investigations often utilize PRTK tool to access password-protected files. Most IT directors and IT team often adopt solution programs to recover system passwords, administrative, personnel lost passwords. PRTK is limited because it runs on a single network system.

Distributed Network Attack (DNA) enhances multipart unlimited operations, and can operate on multiple systems and provide access to passwords for many popular software applications.

Rainbow Tables (RT) are massive sets of pre-computed tables filled with mix up values that are pre-matched to possible plaintext passwords. RT often allow hackers to reverse the hashing function to determine under plaintext types password on the systems and identify two different passwords in the same hash function. The hackers can also identify original password of the system with same hash function. RT is password's worst nightmare and as a result the RT often uses encryption key to ensure that actual password is never sent in clear text across the transmission and communications line.

Brute-Force Attacks (BFA) is a trial-and-error method used to obtain personal identification numbers (PIN) from users. BFA uses automated software to generate many consecutive guesses to access desired data and information. It is often used by cybercriminals to crack encrypted data and security analysts to test individuals and organization's network security. Per Harris and Ham (2016), BFA is an attack that continually tries different inputs to achieve a predefined goal used to obtain credentials for unauthorized access to organization system. Furthermore, BFA is an attempt to uncover password that uses intruder employee sequences of tactics to uncover the correct password. In other words, BFA is an attempt to recover a cryptographic key and password by trying every possible key combination until the correct key is recovered. DNA and PRTK are integrated with Rainbow Tables (RT).

CIAV is an acronym for the four fundamentals of system security which are confidentially, integrity, availability and vulnerability. Most cybercriminal activities are often link to the violation of CIAV triad. Education, understanding and recognition of these four security principles will help cybersecurity professionals to implement effective security measures to protect organizations against cybercriminals (McMillan and Abernathy (2014).

Confidentiality limits access of data and information to authorized users and protects organization against the authorized disclosure of available data and resources. Regrettably, current post-cybercriminals do not have to enroll in college to learn covert leisure pursuit used to destabilize organizations and vulnerable population.

Integrity is the act of insuring that data and information has not been indecorously modified and changed. Perpetrators often have higher advantage in attempting to modify organization data and information. Most organization data and information must be accurate and reliable.

Availability is the act of entrusting access of data and information under the control of authorized users. Vulnerability is a combination of absence and weakness of hardware, software, devices and security plan that leaves an organization's network system open to cybercriminals, cybersecurity threats, damage and destruction of data and information.

Vulnerability is the most unpopular segment of CIAV. Vulnerability provides unrestricted access to an organization's data information and folders on the network system. Most private and public organizations are strongly encouraged to implement countermeasures mechanism to identify and protect against vulnerability activities. A balanced approach to scuffle cybercriminals is to ensure that no facet of CIA triad is abandoned.

Archetype of computer forensics

The world population is changing at a rapid pace. As such individuals, higher education institutions, public and private organizations must consider computer forensics measures to provide in-depth defense against the looming cybersecurity threats. Any attempts to relax or undermine the impact of computer forensics can create a damaging effect on the organization system including the risk of losing important data, files and documents in the system. Types of data collected in computer forensics approach are persistent data stored on a local hard drive and other devices. These data are often preserved when the computer is powered off and volatile data is stored in transit which could be lost when the computer loses power or is turned off. Volatile data resides in registries, cache, and random-access memory (RAM). Volatile data is ephemeral and vital for investigating teams.

As Nnelson (2004) posits, system administrators and security personnel must be trained on the impact of routine system audit and how these data can affect the forensic process, the potential admissibility of evidence in court, subsequent ability to recover data that is critical to the evidence in court of justice in accordance with legal standards. The crucial point for forensics investigators is that evidence must be collected in a way that is legally admissible in a court of justice.

Increasingly, laws are being passed requiring organizations to safeguard the privacy of personal, making it obligatory or necessary for organizations to complying with computer security best practices. Most organization often add computer forensics capability to their current arsenal to submit proof of security policy to avoid lawsuits and regulatory audits. Protection against unreasonable search and seizure, and the Fifth Amendment which allows for protection against self-incrimination. Violations of any one of these statutes during the practice of computer forensics could constitute a federal felony punishable by a fine or imprisonment. Per Eastton (2011), the United States Federal rules of evidence about hearsay, authentication, reliability, and best evidence must be understood. Two areas of legal governance affecting cyber security actions in the United States relating to collect network data deal with authority to monitor and collect data that is admissible in court. The United States Constitution and Statutory Laws govern the collection process, while the Federal Rules of evidence deal mostly with admissibility of evidence in court. System administrators must possess technical skills and ability to preserve critical information related to suspected security incident in a forensically sound manner, relating to legal issues, forensics analysis, response and presentation of evidence in court. As Jones, Bejtlich, Rose (2006) noted, scopes of the forensic investigations and analysis often include identifying malicious activities relating to 5Ws: Why, When, Where, What and Who is perpetuating threats of cybercrimes and line of legal responses. The responses to these series of questions determine whether law enforcement officers and investigating team are needed in the process and if court permission is needed to conduct forensics investigations. Per Nelson (2004); Jones, Bejtlich, Rose (2006) and Gerrain (2017, enlightening guideline in conducting computer forensic investigation must include proactive measures involving:

* Gathering information by assessing the crime scene incident relating to the severity of the incident;
* Identifying the impact of the investigation using information; technology Subject Matter Expert. The SME is a self-guided computer forensic programmer confirming individual's progress per response to answers and questions and if chosen for crime scene incident, response will vary depending on types of incidents and location (Johnson (2011).
* Obtaining information networks system, network devices, router, switches, hub, network topology documentation, computers, servers, firewall, network and crime scene diagram; Categorizing

external storage devices including pen drive, flash drive, external hard disk, CD, DVD, memory cards and remote computer;

* Identifying the forensic tools which can be used during investigation
* Capturing live network traffic to eradicate suspicious activities still on the crime scene;
* Documenting activities during the investigation that can be used in court to verify the course of action following the investigation;
* Imaging the target devices' hard drive and hashing them with MD5 for data integrity. **MD5** is a message-digest algorithm widely used in cryptographic hash function capable of producing a 128-bit (16-byte) hash value and typically expressed in text format as a 32-digit hexadecimal number. **MD5** has been utilized in a wide variety of cryptographic applications, and is also commonly used to verify data integrity (Shinder, 2002).
* Implementing case-management procedures to include the nature of the crime, court dates, deadlines, victims, law considerations and volatile nature of the evidence;
* Differentiation of incidents reports; ranging from low-level (incident is least harmful), mid-level (somewhat serious incidents) and high-level (severely serious incident).

Safety recommendations will be used to implement policies and procedures on workstations and centralized file servers to block executable files from unwanted application programs. To enhance continuous security and safety of information and data on a computer and Abode Reader, Microsoft Windows Autorun and Abode Reader should always be turned off. Another measure to protect machines from attacks hidden in PDF files via hardening is to turn on enhanced security in Adobe Reader. Mail security and gateway blocking effectiveness should also be performed frequently to identify threats prior to getting into heart of network file server via workstations. This way these measures will reduce if not prevent cybercrimes. Smartphones and mobile devices are prime sources of malware and cyber fraud. The decreased uses of smartphones connections to organization's network system will enhance ultimate security.

Cybercrime is complicated and legally sophisticated. Increasing growth and advancements in information communication technologies demands skilled cybersecurity and cybercrime professionals are increasing because of the sophistication of cybercriminals on vulnerable global societies. Federal, state and city law enforcement officers investigating and prosecuting culprits must be equipped to pleat electronic, physical and digital evidence. Per Brown (2015), and Harris and Ham (2016) studies on investigating and prosecuting of cybercrime, forensic dependencies and barriers to justice and law enforcement officers noted that private detectives, uniform and plainclothesmen investigators assigned to cybercrime scene must be entrenched with soft and hard skills, and ability to apply the skills and knowledge in a crime facility.

Chapter 1-B: Professional Engagement
Chapter 1: Strengthening Instruction and Learning Endeavors

Per Esin (2017), Chapple and Seidi (2016), Harris and Ham (2016), McMillan and Abernathy (2014), and Harris (2008), strengthening of instruction and learning process must be reinforced through professional engagement.

Phase 1:
What are the advantages and disadvantages of these items (OECD, Trademark, DMCA, COE and Information Technology Risk).

1. Organization for Economic Co-operation and Development is an international organization that helps various private and public organizations to tackle the economic, social and governance challenges of a global economy.

2. Used to protect a word, name, symbol, sound, shape, color and combination of logo.

3. Digital Millennium Copyright Act is the United copyright law that criminalizes the production and dissemination of technology, devices and services used to circumvent access control measures implemented to protect copyright materials.

4. It stands for the Council of Europe that is deep-rooted in the Convention on Cybercrime. It is the first international treaty seeking to address computer crimes by coordinating national laws and improving investigative techniques and international collaboration.

5. Information Technology (IT) risks are categorized into four groupings: Transfer, Avoid, Reduce and Accept the risks. IT director must implement cybersecurity risk measures such as firewall, antivirus and antispam on organization system. In addition, IT

cybersecurity risks can be controlled using countermeasures and mitigated by restructuring procedures, creating barriers against cybersecurity threats.

6. Describe three most important items concerning cybersecurity threats for public and private organizations.

7. Name organizations that are wide-open to cyberattacks and cybercrimes and what measures can be implemented to prevent attacks.

8. Describe existing marked distinction between cybercrime and ex-employee's sponsored hacking and cracking activities.

9. As IT director, you envision a possibility of a major cybersecurity attack against critical infrastructure of your organization network system. Provide a well-conceived short-range and long-range disaster and recovery plan.

10. The impact of high-speed connectivity. It is true that the use of broadband has expanded the scope of the internet connectivity speed across the globe. Unlike analog with limited range of only 56 Kbps; less than federal government regulations and line of considerations and laser uploads speeds indicating higher download and upload speeds ensuring improved performance on individuals and organizations and open-ended access to hackers, crackers and cybercriminals into organization systems. Notably, cable providers of broadband services continue to offer high-speed downloads and often higher uploads speeds ensuring asymmetric capability within transmission process. Apparently, the upload and download speeds are not created equal. As an IT Director, do you prefer higher downloads speeds to higher uploads speeds, and why?

11. Cyberbullying can be ignored if the case is not unthreatening act and prank to the community. Members of the community are strongly urged to take preventive measures against cyberbullying

and to restrict perpetrators from including others name in their playmate list without authorization. Perpetrators can be cautioned by reporting the cyberbullying case to an Internet monitor service, a website monitor and law enforcement unit. Consider the perpetrator to be a close friend and/or close relative, what will be your immediate response to safeguard your immediate family members? Provide the best response to resolve cyberbullying operative mechanism in general and in this above scenario.

12. Provide professional preventing measures against cyberbullying and stay cyber-safe. Stay off-line, stop communicating cyberbullying messages to others, block communication with cyberbullies, report cyberbullying to a trusted family member, stay cyber-safe, avoid posting and sharing personal information on the Internet, such as full name, address, telephone number, school name, parents' names, credit card number and social security number online and with strangers. Consider the above listings and provide a step-by-step process to battle cyberbullying.

13. The world community is entrenched with threats of cybersecurity. What are appropriate measures used and the role of the intelligence to combat cybercriminals? The role of cyber-crime mechanism is growing in a massive rate, prompting the untimely notification of cyber-threat and prevention of cyberattack. Perpetrators are very sophisticated engaging in structured cyber criminal's lifestyle, speaking criminal languages, the permeation of human communities gathering information on the real identity of potential victims. Provide constructive and trusted mechanism, software, hardware, human resources and intelligence, and additional protection devices to combat domineering and large-scale cybercriminals across the globe.

14. Cyber-threats on private, public and government organizations are overbearing and terrorizing vulnerable innocent societies. Circumventing discussing on cyber-threats is a sad miscalculation due to ongoing emergence of the most dangerous and irritating

nature of cyber-threats. Private, public and government organizations need to implement zero tolerance on emerging cyber-threats operations that most private, public and government organizations are not willing to tolerate and are ready to eradicate. What do you consider the best way to handle these cyber-threats?

Phase II: Multiple Practice Exercise
Choose the letter(s) that correspond to the best answer.

1. Provide best description of data integrity:

   a. Detection of information
   b. Detection virous modification
   c. Detection of modification
   d. Detection of accidental medication

2. Identify which of the following is the best practices to reduce brute-force attacks that allow intruders to uncover user's passwords?

   a. Choose a weaker algorithm to encrypt the password file
   b. Lock account for a certain amount of time after clipping level is reached
   c. Increase the clipping
   d. Decrease the clipping

3. What is the name of the machine used by Germany in World War II to encrypt sensitive data?

   a. Biometric machine
   b. Finger-prong machine
   c. Overclose ln machine
   d. Enigma machine

4. What are the four important services often provided by cryptography.

   a. Data, integrity, information and confidentiality

b. Privacy, integrity, confidentiality and authenticity
c. Confidentiality, integrity, non-repudiation and authenticity
d. Confidentiality, password, username and algorithm

5. Identify the two major types of encryption algorithms Symmetric and private key

    a. Network shared and asymmetric key
    b. Asymmetric and symmetric key
    c. Private key and shared key
    d. None of above

6. The university of Calabar in the former southeastern state of Nigeria want to protect the institution's logo from unauthorized use by cybercriminals. Which of the following will protect the logo and ensure that unofficial users cannot meddle with the logo?

    a. Patent
    b. Copyright
    c. Trademark
    d. Trade secret

7. Identify the United States' copyright law that criminalizes the production and dissemination of technology, devices and services that circumvent access control measures implemented to protect copyright materials.

    a. Copyright law
    b. Federal Privacy Act
    c. Digital Millennium Copyright Act
    d. Portrait Act law

8. Identify the primary international treaty seeking to address computer cybercrimes by coordinating national law to improve investigation measures and international alliance.

    a. Council of Global Convention on Cybercrime
    b. Council of Europe on Convention on Cybercrime
    c. Organization for Economic Co-operation and Development
    d. Organization for Cybercrime co-operation and development

9. The IT director in charge of Saint Paul's Primary School and UDA Community High School at AFI-UDA network systems has been tasked with implementing many security controls such as antivirus and antispam programs to protect the two-institutions' email and the Internet systems. What type of approach is appropriate to the risk posed in the process?

    a. Risk acceptance
    b. Risk avoidance
    c. Risk mitigation
    d. Risk transference

10. Who is the ideal official to approve the organization's technology continuity plan?

    a. Chief Information Officer
    b. Chief Executive Officer
    c. Chief Operation Officer
    d. Chief Financial Officer

11. What method or devise can be used to identify cyberattacks that require sizeable amount of skills?

    a. Dictionary
    b. shoulder Surfing
    c. Social engineering
    d. Birthday

12. Which of the United States standard was developed to secure message digests?

    a. Data signature standard
    b. Data encryption standard
    c. Secure hash algorithm
    d. Digital signature standard

13. What is Cipher Lock?

    a. A lock that utilizes cryptographic keys
    b. A lock using keys that cannot be reproduced
    c. A lock that uses a keypad
    d. A lock that uses a token and perimeter reader

14. Most application programs can transmit over one physical medium at the same time using one of the following:

    a. Routing
    b. Synchronous protocols
    c. multiplexing
    d. Asynchronous protocols

15. Matthias Akuda installed a freeware photo on his computer so that he can manipulate his vacation pictures. Thereafter, he witnessed advertisement pupping up daily on his computer when the utility is in use. The pup up item is known as

    a. Spyware
    b. Freeware
    c. Adware
    d. Malware

16. Which of the following disaster recovery operation is most intrusive for organizations?

    a. Simultaneous check
    b. Daily checklist
    c. Full-interruption
    d. Incremental backup

17. MacEsin is trying to implement reliable authentication system for his organization. Identify the most dependable system for the organization.

    a. Something you have
    b. Something you know
    c. Something you are
    d. Something you have and something you know

18. You have been retained as an IT director for a mid-size organization that has gone through a major natural disaster. What should be done if original facility becomes operational after the mischance?

    a. Contact board members
    b. Move all critical data to original facility
    c. Move most of the critical data to original facility
    d. Let IT team aid

19. Which of the computer components dictates when data is processed by the system's processor?

    a. Registers
    b. ALU
    c. Control units
    d. Buffer

20. What is the meaning of acronym?

    a. Data encryption algorithm
    b. Data encoding applications
    c. Digital encoding algorithm
    d. ALU algorithm

21. Something you know, something you have and something you represents is identified as.

    a. Authentication

    b. Authorization

    c. Availability

    d. Confidentiality

22. Which set of protocols corresponds to the followings layers: applications, data-links, network and transport?

    a. FTP, ARP, UDP and TCP

    b. TFTP, ARP, IP and UDP

    c. ICMP, ARAP, IP and UDP

    d. ARAP, ARA, UDP and TCP

23. Which function is best performed by HAVAL algorithm?

    a. Encryption algorithm

    b. Hashing

    c. Digital signature

    d. Symmetric key

24. Jenco Organization is implementing an access policy based on decentralization operations controlled by administrators and IT team. What are the advantages and disadvantages of such operation?

    a. It puts access control in the hands of those most accountable for data and information that leads to inconsistencies in procedures and criteria.

    b. It puts access control into the hands of IT directors and leads to rigid policy and criteria in the organization.

    c. It puts access control into the hands of executive directors of the organization

    d. It puts access control into the hands of cloud providers

25. Which three of the following items are the organization's technical control systems?

    a. Encryption, Testing and Auditing.

b. Auditing, encryption and networking architecture
c. Testing, auditing, and networking architecture
d. Network architecture, encryption, and testing.

26. Most organizations have specific method of implementing the creation of user's password to ensure authentication. Which of these items best describes the password certification?

a. List of questions for system users
b. Potential cyber-attacks via password
c. Operation that instruct users to create password that are easy to remember and difficult to crack
d. Using DHCP to create personal password

27. Identify two types of one-time password creator token device

a. Event one-time driven
b. Central and decentralization
c. Synchronous and asynchronous
d. Symmetric password operation

Phase III: Multiple Choice Review Answers

1. C
2. B
3. D
4. C
5. C
6. C
7. C
8. C
9. C
10. C
11. B
12. C
13. C
14. C
15. C
16. C
17. D
18. C
19. C
20. A
21. B
22. B
23. B
24. A
25. C
26. B
27. C

CHAPTER 2

Information Technology
Server Security Domain

Domain is the strongest and weakest link in network history. Organizations' Information Technology (IT) directors, managers, and lead-employees have open-ended access to secure, preserve, interrupt and mess up an organization's entire network system at will. Scopes of Domain security violations include human mistakes, internal employees, social engineering and internet protocol (IP), spoofing and spyware (Esin, 2017).

Human mistake –Human mistakes emanate from act of carelessness, lack of knowledge, inadequate oversite and absence of professional training. Most individuals who operate their businesses or work for organizations can intentionally or inadvertently overlook and/or underestimate real cybersecurity threats. Relating to cybercrime, there are broad range of human mistakes often include, but not limited to carelessness and inattentiveness including writing a password on a sticky note and leaving it on the monitor, ignoring warning messages by clicking OK, and/or failing to provide training to employees. Per Johnson (2011), untrained and careless employees are prime targets for cybercrime, cybersecurity threats and malicious attacks and they constitute leading points of entry into the network system.

Internal employees – IT directors and managers who design the network installing, configuring system software, hardware, applications software and security devices are internal employees. Most of these insiders know too well how to bypass security control hiding their track; they also know how to delete logs and time stamps on the network system. IT directors, managers, lead IT employees are in the position of organization TRUST and RISK. Most of the network users are knowledgeable about how an organization responds to cyber-threats and can tailor attack to target unit accordingly.

Social engineering – This involves a psychological manipulation of individuals into divulging confidential information to outsiders or business rivals. Indeed, it constitutes more multipart fraud tricks deployed by cyber-criminals to trick individuals and employees to release user names, passwords, bank information, house and offices' alarm codes and computer accesses to secretly install malicious software and control over the network system.

Today, cybersecurity is recognizing who and the extent of trust and the weakest link in a security operation which may attempt to accept a person and scenario at face value. It may be of no use to install locks, deadbolts, windows, guard dogs, alarm systems, floodlights, fences with barbed wire, and armed security personnel; the system can be vulnerable to cyber security threats from anywhere and at a distance unknown. Deceits behind social engineering arises in three principles, namely intimate relation, pretexting, and monetary value:

Intimate Relation – If a hacker befriends an employee, existing intimate relationship can lead to the employee compromising organization system security.

Pretexting – A hacker can contact one or two employees requesting sensitive information such as passwords and location of organization file servers, firewalls and router configurations, and vital data using texting.

Monetary Value – a hacker can offer an employee substantial amount of money to break through the automated control device like an organization's firewall and/or network system.

Internet Protocol (IP) Spoofing – Spoofing involves changing the packet heads of a message to indicate or pretend that such an IP address is from a legitimate source. The sending computer often impersonates another system misleading the recipient to accept the messages. As Shinder (2002) posits, IP spoofed address is often from a trusted port allowing a hacker to successfully send a message through a firewall and router that can else be filtered out of the system.

Spyware is a software places on individuals' and organizations' system without their knowledge of the host to gather information and send such information to another entity without the consumer's consent.

Seven Domain of Information Technology (IT) Organization

Organizations' network systems of all sizes have millions of transactions occurring every minute of the day among top level administrators, employees, contractors and customers. Amid the growing cybersecurity challenges, organization policies and procedures must include three essential items such as, (1) scrutinizing the existence of appropriate cyber security policies and procedure, (2) corroborating the existence of controls supporting the policies, and (3) confirming effective implementation and ongoing monitoring of the controls system. Today most network systems are automated and capable of generating transactions in the form of online product queries, inventory checks, authorizations, online education, tracking product, service calls, instant messages, airline tickets. Per Johnson (2011) organizations' network system challenges are massive in size, scope and complexity and the preeminent approach to resolving network systems setback is to restructure the network system into manageable segments and domain security accountability. Traditionally, the seven-domain responsibilities ought to include the following: user, workstation, local area network (LAN), wide area network (WAN), LAN-WAN, remote access (RA) and system-application (SA) domains. Segmentation will allow the IT team to follow the flow of the data and information through from end-to-end and minimize the risk of cybersecurity threats (Johnson, 2011; Grama, 2016).

Security Policy: is a policy designed to ensure that risks are reviewed and evaluated throughout the organization's domains and to allow the organization to make a balanced decision. Organization's encounters are governed by various magnitudes of risks and security policy and procedures including data loss protection (DLP) and data leakage protection (DLP) designed to decrease the likelihood of malicious loss of vita data and information. As Johnson (2011) maintains, organizations must deploy strategies to safeguard users and customer privacy as required by law. Various measures must be implemented because hackers and crackers do not have to be physically present to damage the organization's data, files, folders and information, especially if perpetrators are disgruntled personnel of the organization with access to sensitive data and information. DPL often involves members of the organization's executives with access to data and information, especially those who are assigned in the sensitive-data division of the organization. Such individuals could shrewdly and intentionally email entire database to a competitor and their own personal Internet account. Organizations across the globe must implement operational plans of action to protect against potential physical and digital data leaks.

Traditional Network Organization Seven Domains	
Network Components	Activities
User Domain	End-User's authorization to access data, information and available resources in the network system. To protect network system against cybercrime, end-users including current employees, professional consultants and guest.

Workstation Domain	Collection of computing devices used by end-users for job advancement and productivity of organizations. Most devices on workstation domain includes desktop, smartphones and laptop main computer for end-users, but with limited hard drive storage capacity. Most data files and information are stored on organization's centralized file server.
Local Area Network (LAN) Domain	Local area network (LAN) is the backbone of any organization's technology architecture. LAN connects two or more computers within a small region such as home, campus, office and group of buildings. LAN can store limited resources on user's computers using a standard, secondary storage system. Because of growing cybersecurity threats, LAN is considered unsecured.
Wide Area Network (WAN) Domain	WAN covers large geographical areas that consist of several smaller networks and utilizes different computer platforms and networking technologies. The Internet service is a good illustration of WAN. Private WAN (CISCO) can be established to link offices across cities, states, nations and global communities. WAN is recognized as providers of world largest Internet and network services. Because of growing cybersecurity threats, WAN is considered unsecured.

LAN-WAN Domain	LAN-WAN is the technical infrastructure that connects LAN organizations to WAN and allows end-users to access the Internet. Users can use WAN to access LAN anywhere at any time. Access from WAN can be via virtual private networking allowing data and information transmission and communications to flow in both directions in the LAN-to-WAN domain. Because of growing cybersecurity threats, LAN-WAN is considered unsecured.
Remote Access (RA) Domain	Technologies designed to monitor and control how users connect to organization's LAN. Feasible illustration of RA is seen when users can connect to organization's network systems from home computers and mobile devices. Because of growing cybersecurity threats, RA is considered unsecured.
System-Application Domain	System-Application is an important piece of technology needed to collect, process and store data, files and information in an organization's network system. It involves installation and configuration of compatible hardware and software.

User Domain: consists of hardware, software, network communications, protocols, applications, data and information transmission. This domain is implemented within a physical space and includes user interacting with logical and physical features of the system. Delimiting an organization's access into domains usually helps to define limitations and controls the extent of interconnection within the organization's systems. Targets of cybercriminals is on a vulnerable system domain and monitoring. An exploit in one domain often triggers extensive damage on another domain and most end-users are vulnerable and are unaware of the operative components of the organization's policies and procedures. An organization's quarterly professional training on cybersecurity (PTC), control and daily monitoring of network user domain must include the acceptable use of policy (AUP), e-mail policy (EMP), privacy policy (PP) and system access policy (SAP).

Acceptable use policy - It is the implementation of broad-based sets of regulations and standards for acceptable code of conduct when users access file, data, information, resources, browsing Website and personal emails over the organization's domain.

E-mail policy - It is the established sets of rules of what is acceptable when accessing and using an organization's domain.

Privacy policy - This a policy that initiates specific set of rules to enforce the organization's privacy, regulatory landscape and government mandates.

System access policy - This policy created specific rules of conduct for system access, user credentials such identification number, password, software and hardware. Identifying specific roles, connecting employees to specific responsibilities, such as payroll, account receivable, account payable, college and university registrars, logistic managers, sales director and system permission within the roles can help an organization to maintain control access to critical data and information and identify who has access to and uses the network system (Johnson, 2011).

Workstation Domain: Workstation Domain is the backbone of any organization's network system. Users must have authenticated access from user domain to be connected to the centralized file server. Users can be restricted from accessing and using resources from the user domain and users will often be allowed limited rights on the user domain. Workstation domain is often the vulnerable link on any organization's network security process. There can be an experienced and skilled IT Tech-support in the physical control; again, if the users are oblivious of the value of security attacks, the entire network system will repeatedly remain vulnerable to cybersecurity attacks. Users must resist from writing down their passwords, post private, unique items on the monitor and inadvertently downloading malicious software on the organization's system. Most IT directors and IT-Tech-support teams tend to adopt the view that antivirus software is often loaded and run on the system workstation domain. Johnson (2011) posited that organizations' network management team must include the following six objectives in the PTC training curriculum: inventory management, discovery management, patch management, help-desk management, log management and security management.

Inventory management – tracks workstation connection to the LAN and builds inventory of workstations and audit how often each workstation connects to the LAN. Most organization inventory often contains the largest assets; inadequate inventory management report can contribute system malfunction.

Discovery management -- detects software that is installed on a workstation and routine usage. Information inventories are very beneficial when investigating system security incidents to ensure regulatory compliance. Microsoft Exchange Server (2013) is entrenched with built-in role discovery management group, Role Based Access Control (RBAC) with the permission to perform searches of mailboxes in the Exchange organization for data that meets specific criteria and configure litigation on mailboxes.

Patch management - ensuring that current patches are installed and configured properly on the workstations and an area of systems management involving acquiring, testing, installing, configuring of multiple patches on organizations' system. Patch management tasks include: maintaining knowledge of current patches, identifying and installing compatible patches, testing and documenting procedures required for success system operation.

Help-desk management - provides support to end-users through a help-desk. A help-desk technician can remotely access a workstation to diagnose problem, reconfigure software, troubleshoot computer printers, reset user names and passwords.

Log management - extracts logs from a workstation. Log management (LM) comprises an approach to dealing with large volumes of computer-generated log messages. LM covers log collections of users, long-term retention, log analysis, log search and reporting.

Security management - engages in the identification of an organization's assets; including information assets, implementation of policies and procedures for protecting these assets. Security management relates to physical safety of buildings, employees, products, data, information, connections.

LAN Domain: LAN is a trusted zone organization network system connected to a wireless network device known as wireless router. The wireless is a LAN access point (AP) to the Internet. Data, information connection and communications across a LAN are not secured thoroughly. Cybercriminals can detect and detain data going across the LAN network quite easily. This is more easily done if hubs are used instead of switches. Crime perpetrators can simply plug into any network port in the building and capture valuable data and information. Indeed, the use of switches will require attackers to have physical access to the switch to access the network; hence, a switch must be placed in a secured closet. LAN covers a smaller defined geographical area within 3 miles' radius. Operative devices on a LAN include hub, switch, router, firewall, flat network, sniffer and segmented network.

Hub – connects multiple devices within a LAN and a fundamental networking device connecting computers and most network devices collectively. Unlike a network switch and router, hub has no routing tables to broadcast network data and information across each connection. Hub has ports to control the flow of traffic across the network.

Switch - acts like a coin sorting instrument, allowing authorized computer to connect to the network system and duplicate traffics to all ports in the systems. Switch is designed to control network traffic and reduce the chance of cybercriminal intercepting communication. A switch's ability to control and intercept communication is the central advantage over hub.

Switches made for the consumer market are typically small, flat boxes with 4 to 8 Ethernet ports. These ports can connect to computers, cable or DSL modems, and other switches. High-end switches can have more than 50 ports and often are rack mounted.

A Router –It is a networking device designed to forward data packets between computer networks, directing traffic on the Internet. Data packets are often forwarded from one **router** to another within the **networks** constituting the internetwork process to the destination node. A router connects a LAN, LANs or WANs and compatible Internet service provider (ISP) network. Routers are often positioned at entryways where two or more networks connects. Routers use headers and forwarding tables to determine the best path for forwarding the packets; they use protocols such as ICMP to communicate with each other and configure the best route between two hosts.

Firewall -- is a network security system designed to monitor and control the incoming and outgoing network traffic centered on predetermined security rules. Traditionally, a firewall is implemented as a blockade between a trusted, secure internal network and another outside network, such as the Internet, that is assumed not to be secure or trusted. A firewall is a network security system designed to prevent unauthorized access to or from a private network. Firewalls can be implemented in both hardware and software, or a combination of both. Network firewalls are frequently used to prevent unauthorized Internet users from accessing private networks connected to the Internet, especially intranets. All messages entering or leaving the intranet pass through the firewall, which examines each message and blocks those that do not meet the specified security.

Flat Network -- operates with limited control on the network system. When a workstation communicates with another network, the workstation can connect to other network in the system. It is designed to reduce configuration, maintenance and administrative cost and to decrease the number of routers and switches on a computer and connecting devices to a single switch instead of separate switches. Unlike a hierarchical network design, flat network is not physically separated using different switches.

Unlike large network, a flat network is a network segment and Large networks are broken into segments for security purposes, and to improve traffic within the network system. Flat network system is not secure and the use of sniffer can monitor substantial portions of network communication over a LAN.

Sniffer -- can be used legitimately or illegitimately to capture data transmitted on a network. Network routers read every packet of data passed pass through by determining intended destination on the network and the Internet. Routers with a sniffer read data in the packet as well as the source and destination addresses. Sniffers are often used on academic networks to prevent traffic bottlenecks caused by file-sharing applications.

Segmented Network -- a portion of a computer network separated from the rest of the network by a device such as a repeater, hub, bridge, switch or router. Respectively, segment networks contain one or multiple computers. Segmenting a network involves limiting large amount of traffic to a group of computers and eliminating several cybersecurity threats. Indeed, if the system file transfer protocol (FTP) is not properly configured, cybercriminals can use a comfort zone to hack into the network system.

WAN Domain: The WAN Domain provides end-to-end connectivity between LANs. LAN-to-WAN Domain environment includes routers, firewalls, intrusion detection systems and telecommunications components, channel service unit-data service unit (CSU/DSU), codecs, and backbone circuits. In large organizations, WAN is the Internet operation. Most medium size organizations can lease semiprivate lines from telecommunications providers and these lines are semiprivate because they are rarely leased by only a single corporation. The Internet is an untrusted zone and a host on the Internet with a public IP address is at major risk of cyber-attack and also viewed as weak ports and vulnerable. Major security measures are required to protect weak ports in the WAN Domain. Effective IT audit system must be implemented to ensure that WAN is operating in compliance with corresponding policies and standards in order to render data and information transmission and communication secure and private. Implementation of virtual private network (VPN) can create encrypted tunnels on the Internet. Per Johnson (2011) and Grama (2016), creating encrypted tunnel will protect data and information transmission and communication between the workstations from eavesdropping. WAN provides for long-distance communication to extend a network across a wider geographic area. WAN can connect multiple LANs together and transition from a LAN to a WAN often involves some sort of equipment such as a router to forward data between different networks. A firewall is placed between networks and is designed to permit authorized access while blocking illegal access. WAN Domain is considered an untrusted zone, made up of components outside the direct control of the organization, and is often more accessible by attackers.

LAN-to-WAN Domain: is the bridge between a LAN and a WAN. LAN is efficient and effective in connecting computers to network systems. Computers and devices connected to the network must be protected to avoid the risks of cyber-attack. LAN is conventionally a trusted network zone. Communications across a LAN are not protected if connected to outside the LAN. Mischievous employees might be able to capture data going across the network quite easily and especially if hubs are used instead of switches. LAN typically covers a minor demarcated geographical area, but WAN covers a wide-range geographical region. WAN can connect multiple LANs together and transition from a LAN to a WAN by using devices such as a router and firewall. Router is used to forward data between different networks. Firewall is placed between networks to permit authorized access while blocking everything else. To move from unsecure WAN to secure LAN involves segmenting a portion of a LAN into a demilitarized zone (DMZ). Per Johnson (2011), the military uses the term DMZ as a metaphor for creating defense protective zones between opposing forces. The network DMZ is situated outside an organization's network facing the public network and the network file server in the DMZ provides shared-facing access to the organization's Website. DMZ creates tough and hard-hitting measures against network security breaches protecting the organization's file servers from hackers and cybercriminals. To strengthened and secure the organization's network, a firewall is placed between the DMZ and network file servers. The firewall filters traffic from

DMZ servers to a LAN server, allowing limited Internet traffic into DMZ and restricting traffic.

Remote Access Domain – is an enhanced user domain consisting of authorized users with remote access to an organization's resources. Remote access often occurs over unsecured transports such as the Internet and associated unsecured transports such as dial-up via a modem and through, workers mobile access to the private LAN while traveling on the road and working from various locations and home. Again, most often, remote-access relies on VPN, Internet Protocol (IPsec) and Secure Sockets Layer (SSL) to secure connection to the entire network. Most often remote-access relies on VPN to secure access to a public telecommunication and the Internet. It is critical if employees are using a public Wi-Fi hotspot, and compatible devices to connect to the organization's network. VPN can create an encrypted communications tunnel over the network using the Internet. The Internet is an untrusted remote access and subject to cybersecurity breaches. VPN can help to control and reduce the rate of cyber-attack. VPN clients on the remote user's computer or mobile device may connect via VPN gateway to the organization's network. In this situation, employees are strongly required to authenticate their user name and private passwords. Remote access authentication is frequently a major concern when the employee accesses the network from off-campus and less of a concern when accessing the network within the office. Most organizations today indicate that the user name (unique character) and password (unique private character) are not hard-wearing authentication measures to protect the organization's network remotely. Per Johnson (2011), Esin (2017), Murphy (2015), & McMillan and Abernathy (2014) distanced employees should employ two-factor authentication to authenticate their identity using five types of credentials such as something only you know (SYK), something you have (SYH), something you are (SYA), user name (UN) and password (PW). McMillan and Abernathy (2014) further recategorizes password into three classifications: Knowledge factor authentication - something that a person knows; ownership factor authentication - something that a person has; and characteristic factor authentication - something a person is.

Knowledge Factor authentication – This refers to something that only the person knows such as your user name and password combination, and bank debit card. These three private items must not be revealed to anybody. The class of authentication is often providing something that users know and is categorized as Group I authentication such as date of birth, parent's maiden names, personal identification number (PIN). Organization IT directors are expected to implement effective method of continuing review of identification and authentication process of ensuring that users account is current and authenticated, passwords changed at least every 90 days or earlier and disabled after a specific period. An Organization's authentication operation must include the process of creating of passwords, changing and monitoring, and revoking users' account.

Ownership factor authentication - Something that a person has, and these could be devices that you have in your possession, access batch to an organization's building, alarm code to your house and office, remote control code to your garage and security token that flashes a unique number every 10 to 20 seconds and tokens that flash same number twice. Unless you have the correct number, the network cannot be authenticated. The ownership account must include devices such as memory cards, smart cards, synchronous and asynchronous tokens. It is a good practice to recognize that synchronous and asynchronous tokens involve a handheld device requiring the physical presence of the user. It also requires the actual user to be in possession of the device for authentication. The three classes of password authentication is classified as Group II authentication requiring the use of device. Two important stratagems synchronous and asynchronous are utilized for security purposes.

Asynchronous

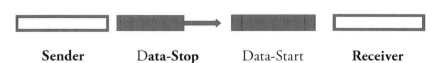

| **Sender** | **Data-Stop** | Data-Start | **Receiver** |

Asynchronous transmission and communication involves start and stop bits systems and the process uses parity bits for ensuring that each byte tends to stop and stop at parity bits. Transmission of small amount of data is often developed and configured entirely through asynchronous device.

Synchronous

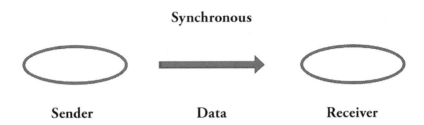

Sender   **Data**   **Receiver**

Synchronous transmission and communication uses a clocking mechanism to synch up the sender and receiver. Data is transferred in a stream of bits with no start, no stop and parity bits. Synchronous transmission often occurs between two devices: a terminal and a terminal server via a clocking mechanism. Transmission of large amount of data is often developed and configured through a synchronous instrument. Group II authentication often includes contact cards, contactless cards and hybrid cards. Contact cards require physical contact with card reader by swiping the card in person on the system; contactless card is a proximity card requiring user to be near the reader and hybrid cards usage involves the combination of contact and contactless cards. Parallel to contact, contactless and hybrid cards and security operation, smart cards have processing power due to the embedder chips and are more reliable than memory, contact cards, contactless cards and hybrid cards.

Characteristic factor authentication - Something a person is such as some type of biometric feature such as biometric passport which is a combined paper and electronic identity document. This type of authentication is known as Group III, a combination of Biometric technology used to authenticate physiological and behavioral characteristics such as physical attribute including iris scan, hand topography, palm and hand scans, retina scans and fingerprints. Digital signature at the back of the passport and driver licensee stored on a tiny computer chip to ensure the integrity of the passport and the biometric data fail with this type of authentication.

User name – unique character

Password -- unique private character and a standard measure of security for individual accounts to access the system, perform the Internet-based transaction and resources.

System Password Configuration

Passwords are limited to individuals. Password authentication varies from one organization to another and are an-open-ended corridor for cyberattacks. Per McMillan and Abernathy (2014) and Esin (2017), individuals, staff members, IT team and leaders of private and public organizations must be prepared and willing to learn and be familiar with diverse types of passwords. Cyberssecurity threats have gone much higher on the list of security priorities across the globe. Perpetrators of cybersecurity threats have raised their dreadful and intimidating fear on vulnerable individuals and private and public organizations. The target against this global scourge is to heighten the understanding, knowledge and awareness of and to reinforce intensive domestic, national and global training on cybersecurity threats. Indeed, based on the frightening rate of violence, cybercrimes, hacking and cracking nature of cybercriminal activities, complication and sophistication of encrypting organization password must not be ignored and/or placed at the bottom of information technology plan.

Standard password - A Standard Password must include a mixture of upper and lower-case letters and numbers. The benefit of such thought-out process is to make easier for users to memorize and remember their password and to prevent cybersecurity breaches.

Combined password - must include a mixture of upper and lower-case letters and numbers and symbols. The advantages of such structured-password are to make it extremely difficult to hackers and crackers to break through and the setback of combined password is that it is difficult to recall.

Static password - involves same password structure. However, it provides a minimum level of security and is often compromised on peer-to-peer network systems.

Complex password – This category of passwords includes a mixture of upper and lower-case letters and numbers, special characters and symbols and often enforces most organizations; policies. The advantages of complex password is that it is very difficult for crackers to penetrate and very hard for most users to learn by heart.

Passphrase password – This set of passwords must include long axiom, making easy to memorize and difficult for criminals to hack and crack. Passphrase is often used to increase authentication system security.

Cognitive password – contains a code word used to verify user's identity including a process of responding to a series of questions relating to the user's personality such as favorite color, mother's maiden name, father's name, city of origin and first school attended. The advantage of cognitive passwords is the user's ability to recall most information and a disadvantage includes the user's inability to remember the original information.

Graphical password – code-named CAPTCHA involves the use of graphics as part of authentication mechanism. Graphic password requires the use of a series of characters in graphic display to ensures that a user is entering actual word, not a robot, and requires password users to select appropriate graphic icon from a list of available graphic arts.

The System/Application Domain: System/application domain comprises of the collection of system and application software and users access to the network. It includes mainframes, application servers, Web servers, operation system software, and applications software. Mail servers send and receive e-mail. Database servers host data accessed by users. Domain Name System (DNS) servers provide name-to-IP address resolution for users. Knowledge within the domain must be specialized. IT directors should focus on specific aspects including mail servers and security ramifications. Application software is the central piece of network operation and can run on a workstation and file server. Most application software is user friendly and can display a screen for users to select the type of data or software needed to get the work done. Servers store data and information in a database for future transaction. System software and application software must be configured and executed in accordance with established policies and procedures by the organization.

Risks and Security Measures: Information security is largely concerned with risk management and IT directors are worried about the risk of cybersecurity threats. Emphasis of private and public organizations are on mitigating risk by implementing appropriate security controls. Individuals, higher education systems, organizations and government agencies often invent credible avenue to design conduits to deal with the risk. Risk begets security threats and risk can be avoided, transferred and accepted. By law, a vehicle is considered a deathly weapon, a luxury item and means of transportation. Driving vehicles on the road, flying aircrafts in the air and operating shipping industry pose countless risks. Consider the risk of losing cars, air planes and boats due to theft and accidents. Most individuals and organizations choose to transfer the risk by purchasing equipment and health insurance. However, other individuals and entities might acknowledge the risk but circumvent the policies by not purchasing equipment requiring insurance. All aspects of human existence are a risk, and naturally vulnerable different threats with tremendous outcome impact individuals, public and private organizations. Most individuals wear a seat belt while driving to mitigate the risk of an accident, most individuals and organizations choose to protect their property with door locks, alarm systems and bulletproof vest. However, some individuals, private and public entities don't.

The global proclivity and vulnerability of cybercrimes have influenced organization's determination, and information technology (IT) directors and managers must be prepared and willing to strengthen each organization's defense mechanism by implementing the enumerated five standard directions to protect organization IT network systems. Grama (2016) and McMillan and Abernathy (2014) posits that organizations are at the risk of losing vital data, files, folders and information if they fail to establish and implement continued IT policy and procedures by designing and implementing the following strategies:

- Designing and configure security hardware, software and devices to ensure safety of organization's data, files and information;
- Providing effective security measures for information technology system within;
- Conducting standard network system inspections and security updates on a regular basis;
- Implementing structured system audit strategies to enhance security policy procedure;
- Establishing and maintaining prevailing information technology security policy procedure; and
- Enforcing compliance through professional training of organization staff members.

Extensive experience and research have revealed that attempts to execute the above standards are often very challenging and aggravating. Unfortunately, most IT teams must be upgraded with modern-day technology knowledge and skills along with the mindset to function as IT team towards achieving perfect security and the ability to implement the same in organizations.

IT Domains Responsibility: The Information Technology (IT) team must keep in mind the importance of an organization's operation and assignment of duties within the structure of the organization based on team members' skills and expertise. It is the responsibility of IT directors to present the well-thought out skills operation to the management. In this modern technology era, auditing and risk management functions are very important and require more training and expertise to map organizational operations into data and information transmission. To enforce accountability, generic or guest accounts are often created for professional consultants by IT director for limited period and such accounts must be monitored and disabled at the end of the assigned duties to avoid security risk. Generic or guest accounts can easily be used to bypass role-based access control into the organization's network system.

Effective organization system auditing will help to strengthen and stabilize information technology operation.

Intellectual property such as backup cartridge and tapes are the lifeblood of an organization. To avoid duplication of copies as private property, system backups are important and must not be performed by a team member with advanced administrative privilege. Authorized backup operators must be appointed and urged to accept and comply with established policy and procedures. Preparing backups designed to protect the sensitivity data and information by using mini-tapes that can easily fit in a pocket or briefcase pose the highest security risk to organizations. These portable tapes could be easily carried out of the organization's premises unnoticed or undetected.

An Organization's compliance to internal and external standards and regulations relative to hardware and software maintenance and upgrades must remain a decisive and definitive solution offering to address the operational goals of that organization. The role of information technology is to accelerate operational procedures or operates to meet the need of consumers' security and compliance with laws and regulations to safeguard data and information. IT directors, managers and team members must implement security policy and procedures at extended high-levels to protect each organization's confidentiality, integrity, availability and vulnerability against cybersecurity threats and breaches. Specific areas of concern must involve the organization's intellectual property, data and information protected under privacy laws, employees' personal information and myriad regulations that organizations must observe a comply with. Frameworks for IT infrastructure must involve following three apparatus: Control Objectives for Information Related Technology (COBIT), International Organization for Standardization and the Internal Electrical Commission (ISO-IEC 27002) and National Institute of Standards and Technology (NIST-800-53).

COBIT -was designed to provide a blueprint for high-level controls processing of data, information systems and technology within the organization. COBIT components contribute to ensuring regulatory compliance, less wasteful information management, improved retention schedules, increased organization agility, lowered operation costs and maintenance compliance with data retention and management regulations. Per McMillan and Abernathy (2014) and Harris and Ham (2016), COBIT components include active involvement in the following:

- Categorizing IT governance objectives and noble practices by IT domains, procedures and linking these objective to organization requirements;
- Identifying process model and common language for authorized users in private and public organizations that often help to map out areas of responsibility, configure, manage and monitor the organization's IT operations; and
- Providing complete set of high-level requirements used to configure, troubleshoot, manage, set up groundwork, control organization IT performance and interrelated functions.

ISO-IEC – ISO-IEC is designed to regulate and integrate security operation into the development and maintenance of data and information security standards published jointly by the International Organization for Standardization and the Internal Electrical Commission (ISO-IEC 27002). ISO/IEC 27002 is pertinent for private, public, commercial enterprises, non-profits, charities, and quasi-autonomous organizations and provide mandatory requirements for data and information security management system (DISMS). The marginal problem relative to the use of ISO-IEC for actual operation rests on the fact that ISO-IEC 27002 is not a standard certification entity; rather, it is a code of practice within DISMS and it is optional and free for public adoption.

National Institute of Standard and Technology (NIST) - sets down standardized regulations applied to private, public and federal organizations. NIST was created and meant to be published on March 28, 2017, but the release was delayed accommodating current internal revision (McMillan and Abernathy, 2014). The Computer Security Resource Center (CSRC) coordinates wide-ranging sharing of information security tools and practices, provides standards and guidelines for resources for data and information security, and to identify key security web resources to support individual users, government, and higher education enterprise users. Per the NIST Computer Security Resource Center (CSRC), major changes to the publication must involve making the security and privacy controls, integrating the privacy controls into the security control, and creating a consolidated and unified set to control organization systems. This will culminate in promoting integration with different risk management and cybersecurity approach lexicons, and strengthening cybersecurity privacy governance and accountability.

Chapter 2-B: Professional Engagement

Per Esin (2017), Chapple and Seidi (2016), Harris and Ham (2016), McMillan and Abernathy (2014), and Harris (2008), strengthening of instruction and the learning process must be reinforced through professional engagement.

Information Technology (IT) Server Domain Security Exercises

Phase I

1. ATI-ASIN has been hired as an IT director and charged with the responsibility implementing standard guideline to protect organization data center.

   * Design, implement and configure security hardware, software and devices to ensure safety of user's data and information;
   * Provide effective security measures for information technology system within basis;
   * Implement structured system audit strategies to enhance security and safety measures; and
   * Establish and maintain prevailing information technology security policy procedure and enforce compliance through professional training of the organization's staff members.

2. Based on my seventeen years in IT industry, I must confirm that attempts to execute above standard is often very challenging and aggravating. Most IT team must be upgraded with modern-day technology knowledge and skills along with the mind set to function as IT team towards achieving perfect security and ability to implement the same in organizations. The team must be ready to:

   * Define the goal of information technology security within a structure organization.

* Differentiate between a cybersecurity threat, cybercrimes vulnerability and organization risk.
* Provide narrative on Filtered Ports or Closed Ports on organization Firewall.
* An IT director must provide steps to prevent a man-in-the-middle cybersecurity attack on the organization.
* The IT director must know and detect the difference between encoding, encryption, and hashing.
* Based on the current technology evolution, the IT director must plan to retain cloud technology for securing organization data and information.
* Where is a demilitarized zone (DMZ) located on the Organization network?
* What are the function of DMZ in organization network?
* Where is a DMZ normally located in an organization?

3. Seven devices on a LAN include hub, switch, router, firewall, flat network, sniffer and segmented network, Narrate specific function of each of these 7-devices on a LAN.

* List Seven Network Domains
* What are the significant differences between LAN Domain and WAN Domain?
* What are the significant differences between LAN-WAN domain and Remote Access Domain?
* What are the significant differences between Remote Access Domain and User Domain?
* What are the significant differences between User domain and System/Application Domain?
* What are the significant differences between Workstation Domain and User Domain?
* Provide specific narrative and contribution of hub, switch, router, firewall, flat network, sniffer and segmented network on a LAN.
* Identify domain with the direct connection to the Internet that enables users to surf the Internet.

- Identify which of the following can be used over Voice over Internet Protocol (VoIP); local area network (LAN), Wide area network (WAN) and metropolitan area network (MAN).

Phase II Multiple Practice Exercise.

1. Voice over Internet Protocol (VOIP) can be used over which of the following?

    a. Local Area Network (LAN)
    b. Wide Area Network (WAN)
    c. Metropolitan Area Network (MAN)
    d. Personal Area Network (PAN)

2. Which of the following is not one of the seven domains of typical Information Technology?

    a. Remote Access Domain
    b. LAN Domain
    c. World Area Network Domain
    d. System-Application Domain

3. What type of access control must be implemented to respond to fixing security incident?

    a. Deterrent measures
    b. Compensating measures
    c. Corrective measures
    d. Detective measures

4. Which of the following laws requires proper security controls for handling privacy data and information?

    a. HIPAA
    b. GLBA
    c. FERPA
    d. A, B, & C

5. Which of the following is not one of the seven domains of typical IT infrastructure?

    a. Remote Access Domain
    b. LAN Domain
    c. World Area Network Domain
    d. System-Application Domain

6. Which of the following are standard IT framework characteristic?

    a. Risk-based management
    b. Aligned business risk appetite
    c. Reduced operation disruption and losses
    d. Established path from requirement to system control

7. Identify the policy that requires employees to lock up all documents and digital media at the end of a workday and when systems are not in use.

    a. Acceptable use policy
    b. Clean desk policy
    c. Private policy
    d. Walk out policy

8. Why is it important to map regulatory requirements to policies and controls?

    a. To demonstrate compliance to regulators
    b. To demonstrate the importance of the security control
    c. To ensure that regulatory requirements are covered
    d. All of above

9. Identify where the organization's sensitive data, files, folders and information normally located.

    a. Data leakage protection inventory
    b. Data leakage protection encryption key

c. Data loss protection storage

d. DLP malware program

10. Which of the following is not a key area of improvement after COBIT implementation System delivery?

a. Decentralization of risk activities
b. Better resources of IT
c. Better communication
d. Data communication

11. What can keylogger software capture?

a. Unique user name
b. Private password
c. Webpage visit
d. Homepage visit

12. Which of the following confirms business access to system data?

a. Data steward
b. Data guardian
c. Data administrator
d. Data manager

13. Reliable sources of organization system security policies, standards and procedures must include which of the following?

a. Government and Law enforcement unit
b. Private hardware and software manufacturers
c. Professional consulting organizations and vendors
d. All of the above

14. Which of the following is not a part of the seven domains of a traditional information technology (IT) infrastructure?

a. Remote Access Domain

    b. LAN Domain

    c. System-Application Domain

    d. Global Area System Domain

15. Organization network system security awareness requires one of the following:

    a. IT Unit

    b. Law enforcement

    c. Shareholders

    d. Customers

16. What type of workstation management techniques help to identify the type of software installed into the system?

    a. Inventory management

    b. Patch management

    c. Security management

    d. Discovery management

17. An organization's on-going monitoring can help to detect and protect which of the following?

    a. System network breach and hackers probing in the network system

    b. Hackers probing in the network system and IT search for crackers

    c. Crackers stealing data and information and system network breach

    d. IT search for crackers

18. Where is a DMZ usually located?

    a. Inside the private LAN

    b. Within the WAN

    c. Between the private LAN and public WAN

    d. Within the mail server

19. DMZ often separates a LAN from which of the following items?

    a. Telephone network provider
    b. Internet Communication
    c. Mobile network transmission
    d. VOIP upload and download

20. Which of the following items are associated with Kerberos authentication implementation?

    a. A tickets-granting ticket
    b. Authentication service
    c. Users, programs and service
    d. A message authentication code

21. Remote access security using a token one-time password generation is an example of which of the following?

    a. Something you have
    b. Something you known
    c. Something you are
    d. Two-factor-factor authentication

22. Identify the ISO-IEC standards and guidelines of an overview and vocabulary of information security management.

    a. ISO-IEC
    b. ISO-NIST
    c. Six Sigma
    d. Identity

23. Identify the purpose of a retina scan biometric.

    a. Examines the pattern, color, and shading of the area around the cornea
    b. Examines the pattern of blood vessel in the eye

    c.   Examines the patterns and records the similarities between an individual's eye

    d.   Examines the geometry of the eyeball.

24. Which if the following can IT team use to segment the LAN?

- Routers and Firewalls
- Routers and Gateways
- Gateways and Subnets
- Workstations and File Servers
- Doman's and Servers

Review Answers

1. A & B
2. D
3. C
4. D
5. C
6. E
7. B
8. D
9. C
10. C
11. B
12. A
13. D
14. D
15. B
16. D
17. A & B
18. B
19. B
20. B
21. A
22. A
23. A
24. A

CHAPTER 3

Institution of Health Insurance Portability and Accountability Act (HIPAA)

Health Insurance Portability and Accountability Act, (HIPAA) was enacted by the United States Congress and signed to law by President William J. Clinton in August 1996. HIPAA's operations ensure that individuals and employees migrating from one healthcare plan to another will have continuity of coverage and will not be deprived of coverage under preexisting conditions. It strengthens the federal government's fraud enforcement authority in various states and regions. Per Murphy (2015) and Muhlbaier (2003), HIPAA's Omnibus Rule of September 23, 2013 allows organizations, professional healthcare consultants and contractors to be held liable under HIPAA laws. Notably, major components of HIPAA laws are privacy and security of patients records and confidentiality of their protected health information (PHI). Lapses in HIPAA laws of August 1996 that was decreed in September 2003 is entrenched with enforcement explanation by covered entities.

HIPAA privacy rule demands compliance, protection of individuals and healthcare entities' right to control unauthorized access and disclosure of patients' PHI. HIPAA security rule requires covered entities control all-inclusive measures to keep healthcare data and records confidential. As Muhlbaier (2003) posits, privacy requires security and HIPAA security standards and regulations were integrated to complement privacy measures and security regulations, covered entities must store healthcare data, information and records in locked files compartments. Intentional and unintentional disclosure PHI often include larger fines and jail time and cybercriminals' violation's HIPAA rule can result in criminal sanctions.

Cyber security professionals are not law enforcement officers, medical officers nor government agents. Cybersecurity officers are required to acquire thorough understanding of the impact of law relative to security operations. As Harris (2008) noted, the world community, medical and educational institutions are becoming threatened using technology in all façade of operations. In response, most countries including the United States enacted aggressive Federal Privacy Act (FPA) in 1974, Gramm-Leach-Bliley Act (GLBA) in 1999 and Health Insurance Portability and Accountability Act (HIPAA) in 1996, Patient Protection and Affordable Care Act (PPACA) and Health Care and Education Reconciliation Act (HCERA) in 2010 commonly known as Obamacare, Computer Fraud and Abuse Act (CFAA) in 1986, Sarbanes-Oxley Act (SOX) in 2002, Federal Intelligence Surveillance Act (FISA) in 1978, Electronic Communications Privacy Act (ECPA) in 1986, Computer Security Act (CSA) in 1987 and Communication Assistance for Law Enforcement Act (CALEA) in 1994. These fully enacted laws and regulations require vital data and information must be accurate, kept up-to-date and must be disclosed to most third parties and associates, allow modification and changes to data and information without authorization by statute and consent of original entity. Technology has increased the scale of data warehouse, data mining and data analysis techniques and distribution all mined data and information.

The Sarbanes-Oxley Act (SOXA) – named after the author was enacted in 2002 in the wake of cooperate scandal and fraud costing investors billions of dollars and threatened to challenge and possibly destabilize the nation's economy. SOXA often focuses on misappropriation of financial operations and an organization's method of reporting their financial status. SOXA provides credible requirements to guide an organization's method of tracking, managing and reporting their fiscal management report, such as safeguarding data and information to guarantee confidentiality, integrity and authentication of all annual reports. Any organization's failure to comply to SOXA often leads to inflexible taut and penalties.

Health Insurance Portability and Accountability Act (HIPAA) (1996) is a mandatory federal government regulatory process designed to protect national orthodox, procedures and standards for storing and/or for transmitting of personal medical and healthcare data and information to unauthorized entity. Fundamentally, healthcare facilities unlike traditional organizations, are often lagging or laxed in data, information and network security-mechanism. Until the implementation of HIPAA, healthcare industries did not recognize personal and any organization's data and information security as a mission-driven mechanism (Hoyte, 2012). HIPAA's stiff regulations often provide a credible framework and guidelines to guarantee the security, authenticity, integrity, privacy and confidentiality of personal and any organization's medical information. Personal and organization's medical records are often defenseless and can be exposed to become easier conduit to unauthorized users in the process of migrating from a paper-based system to an electronic system. HIPAA is mandated to enforce federal penalties for across the state and nation noncompliance healthcare entities, and balanced enforcement by the Office of Civil Rights of the Department of Health and Human Service.

Gramm-Leach-Bliley Act (GLBA) (1999)– This act is enforced through commanding impact on financial institutions, including banks, loan and insurance organizations and credit card providers. GLBA creates a framework for securing financial data and information and unbending procedure against exposing and sharing financial data and information with third parties (Grama, 2016). GLBA allows the board of directors to be the sole custodians of any organization's security, financial operations, risk management framework architecture, security measures.

Computer Fraud and Abuse Act (CFBA) – designed to affect organizations engaged in hacking and cracking protected computers. McMillan and Abernathy's (2014) and Harris's (2008) assessments on regulation and compliance of CFBA of 1986 indicated that CFBA was conceived in 1989, 1994, 1996 and 2001 as the Uniting and Strengthening American by providing Appropriate Tools Required to intercept and obstruct terrorism in accordance with United States Patriot Act in 2002 and in 2008 by the Identity theft enforcement and Restitution Act. Most protected computers, devices and mobile phones are often used by financial organizations, government agencies and educational institutions and must remain under the jurisdiction of the laws. The GFBA prohibits and considers as federal crimes the unauthorized accessing of an organization's and government computers systems to secure confidential data and information, intent to defraud, causing transmission of program, trafficking computer passwords and transmission of communication containing threats causing damage to a protected computer and networks systems.

Federal Privacy Act (FPA) (1974). FPA provides guidelines on collection, maintenance and dissemination of personally identifiable information (PII). FPA was enacted to protect documents of specific branches of federal government including executive, government agencies, independent regulatory organizations and government controlled organizations. Traditionally, the FPA dictates that private and public organizations cannot disclose data and information without written permission and official authorization.

Federal Intelligence Surveillance Act: The **FISA** was designed to provide law enforcement officers and intelligent agencies with systematized measures for physical and electronic surveillance and collection of national intelligence and foreign intelligence information between international communities.

Electronic Communications Privacy Act (ECPA) - designed to enable law enforcement officers, intelligence agencies and structured government restrictions on wiretaps of telephone communication and transmission of electronic information from the protected computer system.

Mythology of HIPAA

The Health Insurance Portability and Accountability Act (HIPAA) was designed to provide privacy standards for healthcare to protect patients' medical records and health information provided by medical doctors, hospitals and health care providers. After the terrorist attacks in New York City, Pennsylvania, and Washington, DC, on September 11, 2001, the United States Congress enacted the Patriot Act in 2001 and the Homeland Security Act in 2002. The passage of these two acts, followed by the implementation of the HIPAA privacy rule on April 14, 2003, led to confusion with caregivers requesting protection from public health departments (PHD), law enforcement agencies and federal agencies. HIPAA was enacted by the United States Congress and signed to law by President William J. Clinton in August 1996. HIPAA law was designed to allow people to keep health insurance, protect the confidentiality, security of healthcare information and empower the healthcare industry to assume full control of administrative costs. The **HIPAA is not Territorial,** but a nationwide healthcare insurance and can often be enforced across the continental fifty (50) states in the United States. As Murphy (2015) posits, HIPAA's Omnibus Rule of September 23, 2013, does not only allow organizations, professional healthcare consultants and contractors to be held liable under HIPAA laws, it also describes the specific responsibilities and profiles of each layer of healthcare providers:

Healthcare Professionals	Job Role in Healthcare Industry
Nurse Aids (NAs)	Provide quality patient care in variety of healthcare settings from physician clinic, hospital system to long-term care environment. Additional role includes moving, repositioning and lifting patients. Education level of most Nurse aid assignment is a high school diploma and completion of state required competency examination.

License Vocational Nurses (LVNs) and License Practical Nurses (LPNs)	The acronym LVN or LPN is used depending on the states of origin. Some states tend to classify this as LVN or LPN. For example, in the state of Missouri, they are known as LPN and in the state of Texas, they are identified as LVN. They must complete a year-long certified education program, take and pass the professional licensing examination. LPN and LVN are represented in most area of the hospital. They play key role in educating patients and the, public about healthcare status, post discharge instructions and variety of healthcare related concerns.
Registered Nurses (RNs)	RNs are in the front line of patient care. They work directly with physicians and other healthcare professionals. Most of their assigned duties include educating patients and the public on healthcare status, post discharge instructions and variety of healthcare related concerns, under the directive of physicians. They work in the same healthcare facilities as other nurses, because of their educational training and professional credential; they can work independently in nontraditional healthcare settings including higher education system, correctional unit and prison. All RNs must be licensed and pass a national RN national licensing examination.

Nurse Practitioners (NPs) and Certified Registered Nurse Anesthetist (CRNA)	For explicit reason, NPs have evolved over the years. Researchers such Johnson (2011) and Grama (2016) posited that NPs emerged because of modern technology, healthcare staffing shortages, advances in technology and a combination of all health factors. Nonetheless, inside the nursing profession, two sets of nurses emerged: nurse practitioner (NP) and the certified registered nurse anesthetist (CRNA). NP and CRNA often play a key role in educating patients, and the public on healthcare status, post discharge instructions and variety of healthcare related concerns. To become NP and CRNA, a person must first be a RN and proceed to advanced classroom and clinical training to be credentialed as NP or CRNA. Their role in healthcare industry may be unlimited: they often operate under the directive of the physician. Depending on the area of specialization, added value for NP and CRNA includes serving in or as customary practices, family practice, geriatrics, OB/GYN, oncology, dermatology and pain management. They can prescribe medications and make referrals under the directive of the physician.

Physician Assistants (PA)	PAs often assume traditional roles and responsibilities earmarked for physicians to help in increasing availability of care for patients. PAs must complete a bachelor of science degree in biology, chemistry, physics or science related areas, two years rigorous PA curriculum in a regional accredited college or university. The process is similar to physician gaining specialty rotations but much shorter in length of time. PAs have proven instrumental to healthcare industry and are recognized as irreplaceable healthcare professionals with license to practice medicine under the directive of a physician.
Physicians (MD)	The role of physician has been proficient and skillful as far back as time of Hippocrates around 350 BC. Physicians are responsible for patients' health condition and treatment ranging from diagnosis, to treatment of injuries and operations in line with their specialization and expertise. Physician obtain a bachelor's degree and four years in regional accredited medical school, and must complete on-the-job training (internship) for a year under experienced medical doctors. Like LPN, LVN, RN, NP and CRNA, physicians must be licensed to practice and hold credential of medical doctor (MD), doctor of osteopathic medicine (DO).

Pharmacists	Pharmacists are members of the health care team directly involved with patient care. Pharmacists undergo university-level education to understand the biochemical mechanisms and actions of drugs, drug uses, therapeutic roles, side effects, potential drug interactions, and monitoring parameters. Pharmacists must undergo rigorous university-level education to understand the biochemical mechanisms and actions of drugs, drug uses, therapeutic roles, side effects, potential drug interactions, and monitoring parameters
Emergency Medical Technician (EMTs)/ATs	EMTs are clinicians, trained to respond quickly to emergency situations regarding medical issues, traumatic injuries and accident scenes. Under the British system, they are known as ambulance technicians (AT), and in most advanced countries like the United States system, they are considered emergency medical technicians (EMT)
Social Workers	Social work is an established professional discipline designed to play a key role in serving patients in healthcare facilities, student in the education system, children, adults and families to control and improve conditions of life and standards of living where individuals' security, safety and ability to participate in civic life are restricted. Currently, there are approximately 84,000 registered social workers in England and 10,000 licensed social workers in the U.S. (NASW, 2004: http://workforce. socialworkers.org)

Psychologist	Psychology is the study of the mind and how it constantly processes thoughts and emotions. Individual's behavior is influenced by the mind's perception of stimuli received through the five senses such as what was said, heard, seen, touched, smelled and often is interpreted and initiates a reaction. Psychologists study the impact of the mind on the body, which is manifested by behavior. Most of them are Medical Doctors and are responsible for providing patient care relative to behavior and mental process.

HIPAA enforceable law plays a very significant role in organizations, higher education system and the healthcare industry. Physicians and allied healthcare professionals are fully aware of the implications and intricacies of maintaining on-site and off-site data storage of healthcare records. Enforcement of HIPAA laws is helping to minimize alarming rates of physician malpractice, overcharging patient's private insurance, Medicare and Medicaid. The recently enacted Omnibus HIPAA Final Rule of 2013 confirms the importance of protecting healthcare records. The HIPAA regulations strictly require covered entities including organizations, higher education enterprise and government agencies to establish and maintain administrative, physical and technical safeguards, ensuring confidentiality, integrity and availability of electronic healthcare records created by the covered entity against cybercriminals and disclosure of patient healthcare information by the covered entities (Heintze and Thielborger, 2016).

Myths of HIPAA: Patients Medical Records

Prior to HIPAA enactment, individuals could get insurance with pre-existing conditions because the previous records were rare to be obtained. However, the emergence of electronic security policies and the invasion of technology in cyberspace has facilitated sharing of medical records. Today, HIPAA is operating on unwieldy set of policies, laws and regulations leading to confusion and misunderstanding by patients and health professionals and can impact patients' domain. HIPAA laws are all-embracing and confusing and most physicians are unsure of the method of approach, and are confused about what can be shared with patients and relatives. Most healthcare providers are not comfortable on how to approach the patients. However, HIPAA laws are elucidated, and translation of the laws are available and posted for review in the United States. Department of Health and Human Services. These laws and documents outline permissions of what to share with patients and relatives.

Patients' privacy is a major concern across the globe. Obtaining required information to perform desired services and sharing same information while maintaining patients' privacy is a trial facing healthcare industries. Most segments of global communities are very concerned about snooping on individuals' privacy. The Holy Bible, Jewish Law, Holy Koran and Buddhist Bible; all have provisions to protect individual privacy and in 1948, the United Nations published the Universal Declaration of Human Rights (UDHR); Article 12 of the UDHR declares that no one shall be subjected to arbitrary interfere with individual privacy (Murphy, 2015). It is imperative for physicians to uphold physician-patient privacy by keeping assessment, diagnosis and treatment of patients as private records and not divulging patient information to anyone. This art of confidentiality can be traced as far back to the Hippocratic Oath (HO) originated since 5th century, B.C. that has survived antiquity and is still moral compass for providing healthcare services. Consent is important action taken prior to releasing medical records to the public. Patient consent is required for gathering, storing and using patient data and information with permission. Patient choice under privacy provides options and is operated between opt-in and opt-out provisions to decrease attempt to disclose any breach of vital information. Under privacy law, disclosing patient information must be based on specific option including health assessment, prescription of medications, treatment, payment and follow-up physician visit. Per Murphy, (2015), HIPAA allows providers to share patient information for purposes of treatment and such information cannot be used in treatment of another patient. Most patients are not mentally and physically capable of reviewing accuracy of assessment and treatment records. Accuracy of patient data, information and storing device of patient records are extremely important in continuing patient care and safety. Today, healthcare systems are targeted by cybercriminals cracking into hospitals, physician clinics and related healthcare storage devices. Medical network systems are infected by malicious software and such infringement places healthcare organization systems and information at risks of being compromised. Keys to protecting healthcare data and information is influenced by data breach. Breaching healthcare system storage network by criminals using malicious software can lead to losing patient data and information, losing huge revenues if patients choose to switch to another contender and bad publicity for organization.

Myths of HIPAA: Patients Privacy

Prior to HIPAA enactment, individuals could get insurance with pre-existing conditions but today electronic security policies have encourage the electronic sharing of medical records.

Hence, healthcare organizations are intensely confused about the principles of PHI with limited attention to cybersecurity threats. Most healthcare organizations fail to see cybersecurity as strategic priority for the security of patients' data, protection of finance information, and as a defense mechanism. Healthcare funding derives from human and technology assets and contribution to make medical assessment and treatment conceivable. Information security is a business enabler permitting healthcare organizations to expand their services into revenue streams as efficient means to approach healthcare operations of conducting existing business. Healthcare organizations can use practical means to combat cybersecurity challenges, and adopting a managed solution is the right mechanism because it involves less infrastructure, fewer employees, and less lead IT employee to oversee operations security process.

Chapter 3-B: Professional Engagement

Per Esin (2017), Chapple and Seidi (2016), Harris and Ham (2016), McMillan and Abernathy (2014), and Harris (2008), strengthening of instruction and learning process must be reinforced through professional engagement.

Phase 1:

1. **Genesis of HIPAA**
    When did HIPAA Become law?
    August 21, 1996

2. **What does the acronym HIPAA mean?**
    Health Insurance Portability and Accountability Act of 1996.
    What are other names for HIPAA?
    Public Law 104-194 (H.R. 3103) The Kennedy Kassebaum Bill

3. **HIPAA was passed to:**
    i. Improve portability and continuity of health insurance coverage.
    ii. Combat waste, fraud, and abuse in health insurance and health care delivery
    iii. Promote the use of medical savings accounts
    iv. Improve access to long term health care coverage
    v. Simplify the administration of health insurance
        Which Title is "The Heart of HIPAA legislation?"
        Title II Administrative Simplification

4. **The purpose of HIPAA is to:**
    To standardize Health care transactions as well as rules which protect the privacy and security of health information.
    When was the final "Privacy Rule published?
    April 14, 2001
    When was the final Security Rule published?
    February 20, 2003

5. **HIPAA impacted the Health care industry?**
   Standardization of transactions to electronic for administrative and financial health care transactions.
   Unique health identifiers for employers, health plans, health care providers and individuals.
   Security standards protecting the confidentiality, integrity and availability of Individually Identifiable Health Information (IIHI).

6. **What is a covered entity (CE)?**
   Health Plans, Medicare prescription drug card sponsors, health care clearing houses, most health care providers, and Business Associates (BA's).
   How many Titles is HIPAA divided into?
   Identify each Title and define their meaning.

7. Title I - Ensures and enhances insurance access, portability, and renewability for working Americans and their families.
   It Increases the ability to get health coverage when starting a new job It reduces the probability of losing existing health care coverage.
   It helps workers to maintain continuous health coverage when changing jobs.
   It helps workers purchase health insurance coverage on their own if they lose coverage under an employer's group health plan.

8. Title II - Administrative Simplification defines rules for transactions, privacy, and security. Title II provides information regarding prevention of health care fraud and abuse; administrative simplification; and protecting the privacy and confidentiality of patient records and any other patient identifiable information in any media form.

9. Titles III, IV, and V
   These 3 titles involve the various regulatory agencies that play a role in the American health care delivery and financing. These titles are:

Tax-related Health Provisions, Application and Enforcement of Group Health Insurance Requirements, Revenue offsets

10. **Define the acronym IIHI?**
Individually Identifiable Health Information.
Define the acronym PHI?
Protected Health information.

11. **Define the acronym BA?**
Business Associate(s)

12. **What is HIPAA's definition of a "Small" Business?**
Those typically having fewer than 50 participants and less than 5 million dollars in revenues.

13. **What is Privacy Standards compliance date?**
April 14,2003.

14. **What is the Security Standards compliance date?**
April 20, 2005.

15. **What is the ARRA and when was it signed into law?**
The American Recovery and Reinvestment Act. It was signed into law on February 17, 2009.
The ARRA and HITECH Act came into legislation at the same time. What is the HITECH Act?
The Health Information Technology for Economic and Clinical Health Act.

16. **What are the 4 Subtitles of The HITECH Act?**
Subtitle A - Promotion of Health Information Technology.
Subtitle B - Testing of Health Information Technology
Subtitle C - Grants and Loans Funding
Subtitle D – Privacy

17. **Define Tier B Civil Penalty.**

    If the violation was due to reasonable cause and not willful neglect $1,000 for each violation of an identical requirement or prohibition during a calendar may not exceed $100,000.

18. **Define Tier C Civil Penalty.**

    If the violation was due to willful neglect but was corrected $10,000 for each violation. If the violation was identical or prohibition during the calendar year it may not exceed $250,000.

19. **Define Tier D Civil Penalty.**

    If the violation was due to willful neglect and was not corrected $50,000 for each violation except the total amount imposed to a person for an identical requirement or prohibition during a calendar year may not exceed $1,500,00.

20. **What are the Criminal Penalties for misuse of unique health identifiers or IIHI?**

    A fine up to $50,000 and/or imprisonment of not more than 1 year. If misuse is under false pretenses, a fine up to $1000,000 and/ or imprisonment of not more than 5 years If misuse is with intent to sell, transfer, or use individually identifiable health information for commercial advantage, personal, gain, or malicious harm, a fine up to $250,000 and/or imprisonment of not more than 10 years.

21. **ARE BA's liable to Civil and Criminal Penalties under HITECH?**

    Yes. The HITECH Act made this sweeping change.

22. **Does HIPAA allow States' Attorney Generals to recover money penalties?**

    Yes. They can collect money penalties as well as costs of suit and attorneys' fees, on behalf of residents of the state who are harmed by the HIPAA violation.

    Name 8 HIPAA related Organizations.

1. US Department of Health and Human Services (HHS). This is the principal agency for protecting the health of all Americans. Centers for Medicare and Medicaid Services (CMS) (Assigned to the Office of Civil Rights (OCR). CMS provides health insurance for over 74 million American through Medicare, Medicaid and State Children's Health Insurance Program (SCHIP). (Part of HHS). The Office for Civil Rights (OCR). the office of OCR is assigned to investigate all complaints regarding HIPAA. Prior to August of 2009 OCR only investigated Privacy complaints. (Part of HHS). Designated Standards Maintenance Organization (DSMO) - the Secretary of HHS named six organizations to maintain the standards defined under HIPAA.

2. Workgroup for Electronic Data Interchange (WEDI). Established in 1991 to address administrative costs in the nation's health care system. WEDI is a voluntary, public/private task force created to streamline health care administration by standardizing electronic communication across the industry. 2. Washington Publishing Company (WPC). The WPC specializes in maintaining, developing and implementing EDI standards. The WPC is the organization that publishes the guides for HIPAA defined for electronic transactions.

3. National Committee on Vital and Health Statistics (NCVHS) -An advisory committee to the Secretary of HHS that advises on matters relating to health care standards. NCVHS has developed transaction standards for the pharmaceutical industry and are undergoing version changes (ICD 10

4. National Council for Prescription Drug Programs (CPDP). First started developing standards in 1977 with the universal claim form. Transaction between pharmacies

and health plans are typically executed in the NCPDP standard, transactions between all other providers and plans are done with X12 Standards.

23. What does Compliance Date mean?

The compliance date is the latest date by which a covered entity such as a health plan, health care clearinghouse, or health care provider must comply with a rule. The compliance date for HIPAA standards generally is 24 months after the effective date of a final rule. The compliance date for small health plans, however, is 36 months after the effective date of the final rule.

24. What are the 6 DSMO's?

ANSI - Accredited Standards Committee (ASC) X12 Dental Content Committee of the American Dental Association Health Level Seven (HL7) National Council for Prescription Drug Programs (NCPDP) National Uniform Billing Committee (NUBC) National Uniform Claim Committee (NUCC)

25. Define Data Content?

Data content includes the data elements and code sets inherent to a transaction and not related to the format of the transaction. The information within a transaction that has nothing to do with formatting.

26. Define Transaction Standard?

A transaction standard is a set of rules, conditions, or requirements describing the classification and components of a transaction.

27. Protection of Patient Privacy

Protection of patient privacy must include any informal and formal discussion of in public condition in public, turning off unattended computer system containing patient data and information and preserving patient tissue sample in a protected container.

Phase II: Multiple Practice Exercise

1. Francis is the chief information security officer for a college network system and is responsible for safeguarding the privacy of user records. What law most directly applies to his situation.

    a. Family Education Rights and Privacy Act (FERPA)
    b. Children's Online Privacy Protection Act (COPPA)
    c. HITECH
    d. Health Insurance Portability and Accountability Act (HIPAA)

2. What is the correct name for the Public Organization Accounting Reform and Investor Protection Act of 2002.

    a. Kennedy-Johnson Act
    b. GLBA of 1999
    c. Sarbanes-Oxley Act
    d. Affordable-Obamacare

3. Which of the following is based on the privacy objective of using personal information in conformity with organization private notice?

    a. Information privacy act
    b. Generally acceptable privacy principles
    c. Medical authentication privacy principles
    d. Internal board review board

4. Healthcare data and information accessed on a laptop off-site the organization is an example of.

    a. Maintenance
    b. User access
    c. Disposition
    d. Distribution

5. Identify the first step of the incidence response process.

    a. Recovery from incident
    b. Recover from the incident
    c. Detect the incident
    d. Respond to the incident

6. What in the second step of the forensic investigation process.

    a. Identification
    b. Collection
    c. Preservation
    d. Examination

7. Publishing service level agreements on an organization internet The most likely person to operate a magnetic resonance imaging (MRI) device must the following (**Circle only one correct answer**)

    a. Nurse Practitioner
    b. Orthopedic doctor
    c. Register nurse
    d. Medical technician

8. The act of outsourcing health data and information management to third party is known as.

    a. Regulated law in the United Stated not in Canada
    b. Illegal in the United States and European Union and Canada
    c. Covered in leading privacy and security frameworks
    d. Reduces information risk to the healthcare industries

9. In healthcare organization, which of the following impose direct impact on data and information breach.

    a. Increase patient care cost
    b. Share patient data and information
    c. Withholding of medical history
    d. Unauthorized disclosing patient data

10. The governance board that oversees information protection of research is known as.

    a. Data and information governing board
    b. Incident response board
    c. Institutional review board
    d. Employee management board

11. To properly control and manage third-party data and information risk, healthcare organizations must always.

    a. Inventory all third parties that handle protected healthcare data and information
    b. Assign objective clinical team to review all service level agreements
    c. Use the same vendor for all services requiring controlling protected healthcare data and information
    d. Ensure patient consent is obtained including sharing data and information with third parties

12. Notably, the international standard that requiring data collection to meet conditions of transparency, legitimate purpose and proportionality is known as.

    a. EU data protection act
    b. ISO 29100 privacy framework
    c. HIPAA law
    d. Generally acceptable privacy principles

13. Attempt to contract healthcare data and information with off-site provider in known as.

   a. Team augmentation
   b. Public Cloud provider
   c. Community cloud center
   d. Outsourcing

14. The concept allowing an individual who has a legitimate interest in providing information about the process of data is known as.

   a. Access
   b. Transparency
   c. Openness
   d. Accountability

15. To apply software vulnerability patch to organization medical device, which of the following need to be contacted for evaluation and approval.

   a. Biomedical Team
   b. Food and drug administration
   c. Medical device manufacturer
   d. Chief IT director

16. Identify which of the following items is not one of the five rules of court evidence.

   a. Be accurate
   b. Be complete
   c. Be volatile
   d. Be admissible

17. When conducting clinical research, which of following can authenticate that the research presents alternative measures to safeguard protected healthcare data and information.

a. Board of trustees
b. Board of directors
c. Institutional review board
d. Medical board certification

18. Which of the following national developed the personal information protection and electronic document act (PIPEDA).

a. Japan
b. Switzerland
c. Canada
d. Great Britain

19. The orthopedic specialists will focus which of these patients.

a. Foot and mouth patient
b. Ear and nose patient
c. Joint problem patient
d. Oral Language patient

20. Under the United States healthcare law (HIPAA), a data breach occurs when threshold is exceeded.

a. Risk of harm
b. Risk of authorization access
c. Risk of disclosure
d. Risk of patient care

21. What United States law mandates the protection of Protected Health Information (PHI).

a. Family Education Rights and Privacy Act (FERPA)
b. SAFE Act
c. Graham Leach Bliley Act (GLBA)
d. Health Insurance Portability and Accountability Act (HIPAA)

22. The authentic principle of security is often known as.

    a. Confidentiality, integrity, accountability
    b. Contingency, integrity, accountability
    c. Confidentiality, integrity, availability
    d. Confidentiality, interoperability

Review Answers

1. E
2. C
3. C
4. C
5. D
6. C
7. C
8. C
9. D
10. C
11. C
12. A
13. A
14. D
15. C
16. C
17. C
18. C
19. D
20. C
21. C
22. C
23. C

CHAPTER 4

Cloud Computing Technology

Cloud technology provides security defense to the healthcare industry where organizations' network systems are monitored and maintained by a third-party provider. Per Murphy (2015) assertion, most healthcare organizations are resisting adopting cloud technology as solutions that must include compliance to cloud service provider regulations which are reliable, scalable, affordable and meet regulatory requirements. Most healthcare organizations are slowly realizing the important of protecting data and information, local hard drive, alternative centers due to understaffed and underfunded facilities. Cloud providers are increasing scopes of investment in security to accommodate customer concerns by employing the best security tools, well-equipped and trained security staffs. Per Reese (2009), cloud-based technology operation is not infallible and waterproof; rather, it is a dynamic protective and tenable option and more lasting and secure than current one-way healthcare center system. It exits to relieve cost pressures on healthcare organizations, by moving substantial portion of data applications to cloud setting operation thereby securing data and information through cloud technology. Cost pressures, budget constraint and security of data and information have helped most healthcare organizations in re-evaluating of healthcare security centers, redirecting IT professionals from a labor-intensive, penetrating system auditing and updating software programs to smaller agile teams of professionals supported by improved technologies. In this setup, the security services are provided by providers with the expertise to manage increasingly complex systems in ever-evolving security operations. Outsized data applications now serve as contributing indicators for healthcare organizations in making well-versed, strategic security decisions to adopt cloud technology.

Cloud technology data application and storage centers are reliable and able to store and/or retrieve data and information per organization request just as good as lead employees operating these centers and data applications. It is quite certain that if massive data and information are left unattended on only one locale, without intelligent analytics, knowledgeable security professionals, the organization will be deemed worthless to vulnerable clients and healthcare population. Cybercriminals are continually gathering intelligence on cloud technology security solutions with possibilities of gaining reduced-visible communicative patterns to conceal malicious actions. Cloud technology providers must be equipped with expertise to analyze acquired data and information immediately to identify actionable insights to keep criminals out of the central data center.

Operational teams take control of sensitive data and applications, in order to hold cybercriminals at bay and be able to respond to cyber-threats prior to data leaving the data security professionals are greatest healthcare organization's security threats and constitute prime vulnerability breach in the main access points of most organizations; systems. Per Reese (2009) and Murphy (2015), 75% percent of cybercriminals attacks takes few minutes for data ex-filtration, and approximately 50% percent of breaches often stick around for months and upon discovery of attacks, remediation will take undetermined human and financial resources to remediate. Monitoring incoming and outgoing email activities and web gateways will protect and prevent cybercriminals from hacking into healthcare organizations' data storage. Organizations' challenges will include rewriting and sandboxing suspicious universal uniform locator (URLs) to detect drive-by cyber-attacks, deploying authentication, endpoint and gateway controls to share information relating to the coordinated reduction of cybercriminal attacks. Organizations are combatting challenges relating to the chasm created between traditional hard drive data storage and cloud technology data facility hosting vital data in a foreign and far-off data storage. As Reese (2009) noted, real-world setback on outlying cloud technology operation center often occurs if:

- Cloud providers declare bankruptcy, obliging storage data centers to cease to operate and control possibly handed over to competitors;
- Competitors do not recognize current clients' contractual agreements, sue cloud providers to obtain a blanket subpoena granting unlimited access to cloud clients' servers; and
- Cloud fails to provide proper security in maintaining physical infrastructure and adequate access resulting in compromising clients' data.

The nucleus of healthcare organizations 'well-being is patients' records and data and guaranteed solution to this safety, regardless of data location, is to implement encryption of data and network communication, encryption data backups and on-site and off-site procedures to safeguard the organization's data and information. IT Directors and lead IT employees must be prepared to create structures where historical data can be retrieved and recovered if cloud technology provider's close and vanish from the face of the planet. Bring -your-own-device (BYOD) in healthcare organization is at epidemic magnitudes and most patients prefer using Apple MacBook, iPads, Android tablets, and smartphones to protect vital data and information. Healthcare leading customers and physicians who know risks have declined this method and resorted to using standard Windows laptops for official health assessment, diagnosis, treatment and prescriptions sent to patient's pharmacy. Mobile applications used by healthcare teams contain the organization's and patient's vital data and continued usage of configured personal devices often expose organization network operations to security risks. 98% percent of application programs written for Android platform contain gaping security vulnerabilities, unsafe practices, and most IT professionals often do not have skilled personnel and resources to mitigate the network operation (Reese, 2009). Since BYOD and mobile threats change constantly due to the proliferation of new mobile applications, healthcare organizations must incorporate adaptive technologies to manage identities, and control and monitor data access. Cyber-criminals repeatedly use mobile devices to launch attacks and to neutralize predetermined sophisticated threats. As a result, IT professional teams must establish network visibility operation, intelligence and efficient response, collaborative alliance and information sharing partnership amongst healthcare organizations and patient's population. Privacy data and information must always be protected. Confidentiality of organization data and information varies depending on the organizations, entity and locations covered and the mystery behind privacy of data is open for deliberation and conformation of what constitutes privacy of patient data. Per American Institute of Certified Public Accountants (AICPA), established in 1887, privacy management is the rights and obligations of organizations to collect, protect and retentions of personal and financial information. Privacy of patients, data in healthcare industry and clients in organizations often include the following:

1. Full Name
2. Addresses
3. Employees' name
4. Relatives' name
5. Patients' name
6. Date of operation
7. Time of operation
8. Telephone number
9. Driver license
10. Fax numbers
11. E-mail addresses
12. Social Security Numbers
13. Medical record numbers
14. Patients' and Clients' Identifications
15. Voiceprints
16. Fingerprints
17. Full face photos

Benefits of Cloud Computing Technology

Cloud computing technology is often fast and allows small and medium size organizations to strive alongside with large corporations. It also enables all sizes of organizations to operate using large external hard drive accessing community information anytime, and anywhere. Most healthcare organization network files servers often have redundancies designed to endure typical hardware problems. These organizations and retain and manage network files servers and protect them against hardware malfunction, power outages, system failure, flood, hurricane, extreme cold and heat, ongoing upgraded, hardware and software installations, configurations, troubleshooting and regular network maintenance. Managing and maintaining traditional network files servers is frequently an overwhelming and a task-oriented process that helps to free most organizations from underlying hardware, software installation and software application upgrades, auditing and management. Rapid growth and advances of cloud computing technology relating to the Internet-based devices and services is causing healthcare organizations to give a serious thought about data, information security; hence healthcare stakeholders and managers must take steps to control, protect and secure current and future data and information.

As Reese (2009) and Castaldo (2015) noted, contract entities must ensure that their own storage facility, customer data and information are protected when sharing or not sharing. Gramm-Leach-Bliley Act (GLBA) and the Health Insurance Portability and Accountability Act (HIPAA) requires covered entities to protect data and information of all patients (Murphy, 2015 and Muhlbaier, 2003). Most healthcare organizations are rapidly moving toward cloud computing technology because it is a reliable resource of storage and the shared storage is accessible through the Internet. However, these healthcare organizations are adopting cloud computing technology storage settings from outmoded storage environments organized for singular-purpose network file server storage systems. Traditional hard drive storage often results in untimely breakdown, low service utilization, gross inefficiency, and inflexibility in responding to organization's desire for stable and continued network operations. Cloud computing technology is a promising and attractive storage environment for healthcare and organizations in need of alternative and reliable storage system for privacy and security of patients' data and information. Remarkably, cloud computing technology environment is designed for multiple organizations intermingling within the same architecture, consumers and financial institutions, educational enterprise and government agencies.

The United States healthcare organizations are obliged to comply with regulations and standards set forth by HIPAA based on cloud computing storage. The United States healthcare system has recognized and accepted HIPAA laws as a reliable trans-border security and privacy policy set forth to protect the population against cybersecurity intimidations and threats. Murphy (2015) noted that the personal information protection and electronic documents act (**PIPEDA**) established on April 13, 2000 is a Canadian law relating to data privacy and how to govern private organizations and disclose personal information during operations to facilitate the efficient use of electronic documents. Most Canadian provinces recognizes and acknowledge existing challenges of privacy and security of clients' data and information, and trans-border sharing of data. Hence, the Canadians were very particular about requiring healthcare organizations to control and maintain data and information within the Canadian healthcare network systems. As Murphy (2015) and Reese (2009) noted, European Union data protection detective (DPD) regulates trans-border data and information transfer and sharing with foreign counties must be approved by the EU authority. The astonishing advantage in cloud computing technology is increased efficiency; services, data and information are rapidly deployed for use in a matter of minutes versus weeks and months of delay. Five traditional benefits beyond efficiency on the use of cloud computing technology include the following:

Business agility - getting the needed computer resources on a scheduled time, ability to deliver results faster through inexpensive operation and quality service that might challenge competitors.

New business models – create a better opportunity for innovation initiatives often generating new value propositions and resulting in new revenue streams.

Less operational issues- establishing traditional standardized service operations to reduce defects, increase business continuity, reduce time spent on unproductive issues and to focus on the mission-driven operation of the organization. Cloud computing technology tends to allow the deployment of the matching topology of services repetitively, with the same result every time and enabling organizations to deploy pre-build file server images, application services and entire application landscapes.

Better use of resources - business agility model often leads to efficient projects and less operational service, allowing customers to spend time on productive activities with greater potential value to the organization. However, benefits differ from one organization to the other, as organizations acquire bigger assets and managerial expertise and progress.

Less capital expense – Most often, an organization's value tends to shift from a capital expense (Cap Ex) model to an operational expense (Op Ex) model. Overall sentiment is that, specifically for short and midterm projects, the Op Ex model is more attractive because there are no long term financial commitments. The Op Ex model often produces zero upfront investment, allowing organizations to start projects faster; ultimately, they end up without losing any investments in the cloud services.

Most cloud computing services are accessed through a web browser like Microsoft Internet Explorer, Microsoft Edge, Mozilla Firefox, or Google Chrome. Cloud computing technology services do not require organizations and users to have sophisticated file server storage on the network systems; rather, cloud is an alternative to hardware and software programs that organizations will be able to traditionally manage in-house and an alternative to hosting managing local data, information and email servers. According to Reese's (2009) assessment, cloud computing technology constituent relationship management (CRM) database system is an alternative to hosting a donor database in an organization's storage center. Four major layers of cloud computing technology include Cloud Clients, SaaS-applications, PaaS-platform and Iaas-infrastructure. Cloud computing layers vary slightly from one layer to the next and generally classified infrastructure as a service, platform as a service, and software as a service.

Layer One
Cloud Clients Web Browser, Mobile Applications,
Thin Client and Terminal Emulator.

Layer Two
Software as a Service (SaaS) Application
CRM, Email, Virtual Desktop, Communication
and Games.

Layer Three
Platform as a Service (PaaS) Platform
Execution Runtime, Database, Web Server and
Development Tools.

Layer Four
Infrastructure as a Service (IaaS) Infrastructure
Virtual Machines, Servers, Storage, Load, Balancers and
Network. Cloud-based Voice over Internet Protocol
(VoIP) telephone service

Software as a Service (SaaS)

SaaS layer is an Internet-based software service available for purchase and rent on a per-user, per-month basis. It is the most common type of cloud service for individuals and small offices. Indeed, SaaS applications are highly customer-oriented and do not require skill and technical expertise for day-to-day operation and maintenance.

Platform as a Service (PaaS)

PaaS layer often provides users with framework and set of functions that can be customized and used to develop applications such as Google App Engine.

Infrastructure as a Service (IaaS)

IaaS is the foundation layer of cloud computing technology set up like storage, backup, and security to include database, storage, virtual private server, and support services that are available on demand by the hour.

Potential Advantages of Cloud Computing

Cloud Computing technology holds a lot of exciting potential for all sizes of private and public organizations ready and willing to realize cost savings through maintaining the organization's server to enable new levels of sharing and collaboration. Cloud computing is created to reinforce and promote greater network system transparency and increased need for effective organization operations, and to break down the barriers in communication and sharing useful information and to enhance effective and durable organizations.

Cloud Computing - Anywhere, Anytime Collaboration

Software program service which acts as a great simplifier for many organizations' storage facilities. Users with off-site authorization connection tend to access the organization's network system and cloud technologies thereby creating easier collaborate with counterparts outside the organization. Cloud computing technology provides users ability for team collaboration such as shared calendars, video conferencing, instant messaging, and file sharing via Office 365.

Potential Drawbacks of Cloud Computing Technology

Cloud computing technology is changing in a rapid progression and the danger relative to cloud technology is that projected host data and information storage are susceptible to going out of business and radically changing the service agreement. A sudden change in service agreement from the host storage is often detrimental to customers. The best cloud computing service is the one that provides users opportunity to access the system, download data and information from anywhere and at any time.

Benefit of Cloud Technology

Organizations are becoming conservative with budgets and reduction in information technology (IT) teams. The process will eradicate purchase of hardware, software, installations, configurations, troubleshooting empowering IT team and organization to become dependent on the Internet connection through cloud technology. Most organization's mission-critical activities are completed using cloud technology, and organizations will need more bandwidth to minimize untimely failures in Internet connectivity. Cloud technology involves the consistent use of Internet access for connection. This dependency may present problems and cloud technology is not the solutions for such organizations. Cloud computing technology is quickly changing and will continue to play an increasingly key role for private and public organizations.

Scope of Data Breach

Data and information breach is a computer-based malady demanding serious attention by healthcare organizations. The reputation of educational enterprises, government agencies and healthcare industries can be damaged by data breach. In fact, data breach often causes patients to loss trust in physicians, healthcare professionals and entire healthcare industry and can result in patient mistrust, unpleasant and negative publicity, loss of current and future revenues and productivity. Data breach is an art of disclosing data to the public without the knowledge and consent of patients, relatives or designated guardians. Healthcare data resides in a dedicated organization's proprietary network file server. Most proprietary file systems are confidential in nature and valuable to organizations. Per Fitzgerald and Schneider (2015), potential grounds triggering data breaches include the following:

- Disgruntled employee's willingness to harm employers by willingly taking information from organizations for malicious purposes.
- Loss of organization laptops and devices containing organization data.
- Infecting organization network file servers using workstations, laptops with malicious program such as Malware to unintentionally share vital data conversations to outsiders.

Cybersecurity Threats

Statistics reveal that a stable defensible professional personnel development (PPD) program on cybersecurity is required in the global community (Bucci and Rosenzweig, 2014). The international communities have benefited tremendously from life-changing cyber-technology, a benefit which was previously only accessed through for the Department of Defense (DOD) and law enforcement officials. As Smith (2015) submitted, department of defense and law enforcement personnel are not the only agency to face the cybersecurity challenges and swift response to emerging cybersecurity threats; all branches of law enforcement agencies, private and public organizations, higher education institutions and vulnerable citizens must be properly equipped with the tools, data and information needed to tactically battle talented cybercriminals. Esin (2017), Smith (2015), Givens (2015), and LeClair and Keeley (2015) in their studies on building the cyber force workshop and conferences support the premise that implementation of PPD will empower law enforcement personnel, public and private organizations, universities, colleges, schools and the global population to expressively strengthen and establish the framework and processes, and to utilize inert human talent required to combat cybersecurity threats. Cybersecurity is a cumulative threat against international communities, and has become a preoccupation of directors of Central Intelligent Agency (CIA), Federal Bureau of Investigation (FBI), Secret Service Agency (SSA), and Cyber Security Technologists (CSE) who have recognized the rising culture and the canon of cyber technology delinquency and perpetrators of cybersecurity crimes. As Easton and Taylor (2011) noted, nine out of ten cases of cyber technology delinquency involve elements of cyber-technology breach not readily visible to technology professionals. Cyber-technology breaches are naturally categorized as abrupt cyber-technology crime because they constitute procedures used to execute the cyber security attack. Per Cross (2008), cyber-technology are classified into two broad confederacies; As Cross (2008), Easton and Taylor (2011), Morley (2013) and Vermaat (2014) asserts, violent cyber-technology crimes are on the rise and postulate imminent danger to global population.

Battling Cybersecurity

Per LeClair and Ramsay, (2015, LeClair and Keeley, (2015), Esin (2016), and LeClair and Rumsfeld (2013), cybersecurity threats and process include the following:

- Cybersecurity threats often distract human intelligence, create vulnerabilities, defy, manipulate and inflict considerable damage to besieged organizations;
- Cybersecurity threat is non-geographical and astonishing, and the consequence of cyber-technology and internet revolution frequently occur unnoticed to human population; and

- Cybersecurity threat is a breach of confidentiality, integrity and availability and stumbling block to organization infrastructure, direct connection, transmission, communication through devices such as switches, firewall, routers, e-mail and Web servers.

Landscape of Cybercrime

Cybercrime is the across-the-globe operation in our generation and out of control. Per Cashell, Jackson, Jickling & Webel (2014), circulation of dollars supports sweeping damage to innocent victims through cumulative effect of losses of data, information and intellectual property. Cybercrime affects hundreds and millions of people who frequent suffer the loss of private property, human lives and money. Cybercrime episodes of 2015, involved the loss of approximately 40 million people in the United States, 54 million in Turkey, 20 million in Korea, 16 million in Germany, and more than 20 million in China. The recorded activities can cost approximately $160 billion per year. Overall, cybercriminals still have difficulty turning stolen data into financial gain and continued global collaborative battle can lead to contributors' ability to put growing cybercriminals out of control. Impact of cybercrime damages often range from trade commission, competitiveness alliance and innovative global economic growth including these four occupational landscapes:

- Cybercrime is on the rise and continue to increase because of large segments of organizations and consumers around the globe frequently connection to the Internet and websites;
- Theft of intellectual property is on the sweeping rise, though equipment manufacturers and acquiring nations and organizations have expanded their ability to slowdown the pace of global innovation and reduce the rate of return to innovators and investors in order to slow down the risk of cyber intrusion.
- Governments need to begin to form serious united fronts of systematic and collaborative effort to collect and distribute data to help developing nations and organizations make informed decision on matters relative to cybercrime.

The cost of stolen Intellectual property (IP) is difficult to estimate and difficult to determine; it is complicated, intangible losses and not easily measured. Per Cross (2008), Eastton and Taylor (2011), and Morley (2013), the average loss of IP among most nations was 0.5% of GDP. Countries in Europe and North America lost more while countries in Latin American and Africa lost less. These disparities are explained in part by the fact that the best hackers prefer to target richer countries. Lack of broadband connectivity often exerts adverse impact on developing nations without broadband connectivity. The overall effect of IP losses is limited on developing countries and significantly increases on developed nations. Well-to-do countries with better defense mechanisms are attractive target to cybersecurity attacks, hackers and crackers while less-developed nations with limited defense systems are vulnerable cybersecurity attacks.

Cyber technology, intelligence sharing, and collaboration is a reliable tool in combating cybersecurity threats and cybercrimes. Intelligence sharing, and partnership is often ineffectively used because of unwarranted government restrictions that tend to interfere with increase on global economy and security of the world population. According to Cashell et al., (2014) and Blair et al., (2014), legal ambiguities time and again slow down collaboration and information sharing and create barriers to the voluntary gathering and dissemination of data and information amongst nations, government agencies, organizations and citizens. As Hoyte (2012) noted, the United States' Congress acceded to the provision of establishing restrictions to help in combating cybersecurity threats, cybercrimes, cyberterrorist through better collaboration, information sharing and restoration of global economy in the aftermath of cybersecurity attacks and cybercrimes. Per Cashell et al. (2014), the implementation of Cyber Intelligence Sharing and Protection Act (CISPA) in 2011, Strengthening and Enhancing Cybersecurity by using Research Education, Information and Technology Act (SECUREIT) in 2012 and Cyber Security Art (CSA) in 2012 have played a key role in preparing the global population in fighting cybersecurity attacks. As current researchers on cybersecurity threats, such as Cashell et al. (2014), Barton et al. (2012), Blair et al. (2014), Lewis & Baker, (2014) and Eastton & Taylor, (2011) emphasize, restriction against intelligent sharing, global collaboration and vital data and information dissemination amongst international communities will empower heartless and cold-blooded perpetrators of cybersecurity to attack and terrorize innocent world populations.

The exponential increase on cyber-crime has inadvertently forced nations, government agencies, organizations, inventors and citizens to concentrate on the impact of global economy in the aftermath of cyber threats and actual attacks on innocent residents and financial damages on all segments of the global communities (Ngwang, 2016). Esin (2016) noted that three major disasters in this century- on September 11, 2001 attacks (code-named 9/11) in New York, Pennsylvania, the District of Columbia in United States, on November 13, 2015 in Paris, France and on December 4, 2015 in San Bernardino, California, United States have helped to reinforce the International awareness of the impact of cybercrime on global economy in all segments of the globe. In addition, the three incidents and other minor ones awakened in nations and citizens an awareness of the reality of the impact of perpetrators of cybercrime and their evil intentions to disrupt the global economy. A close reflection on the three horrified snapshots depicted below clearly confirms the possibility of the loss of many lives during unexpected cybercriminal attacks.

An all-out mechanism to eradication cybersecurity threats and cybercrimes must begin with the world nations, members of executive and legislative branches of the government, private and public organizations getting fully united, and resolute on a common front to confront heartless cybercriminals. The forethought of CISPA in 2011, SECUREIT in 2012 and CSA in 2012 by the United States Congress demonstrates a credible avenue to restore confidence in nations, organizations and citizens, and the determined use of CISPA, SECUREIT and CSA Arts guidelines to eradicate barriers for voluntary information, intelligence sharing and collaboration among nations to combat cybercrimes

The far-sightedness of CISPA, SECUREIT and CSA by the United States Congress to allow information and intelligence sharing was debatable due to the absence of legal procedure, on the one hand, and the fear of the breach and misuse of shared data and information, and intrusions and unauthorized of intelligence sharing on the other hand. As Blair et al. (2014), Cashell et al. (2014) and Esin (2016) noted, most national leaders are challenged and largely unprepared for endangerment of cybersecurity threats to the independences and freedoms of the world citizens. Private and public organizations and government agencies consider misused of shared information with other nations a security risk and vital data and intelligent information often remains locked within organizations due to different concerns and reservations. There is the frequent fear of liability if shared vital information falls into wrong hands, turns out to be wrong and causes unintended damage global citizens. However, this skepticism should not impede the fight against cyber terrorism. Rather, this understanding, arrangement and agreement on intelligence sharing and collaboration should help to overcome hurdles by strengthening individual, private and public organization confidence and trust to cautiously work with the government and legislators of global populations and appropriate national security authorities to eradicate cybersecurity threats and cybercrimes.

Sources of Data

As Blair et al. (2014) and Lewis and Baker, (2014) noted, cybersecurity and cybercrime is a fast-growing industry, where proceeds are rising and benefits are low and truncated, but dangers and damages to global communities are in high-pitch. The likely annual cost to the global economy from cybercrime is more than $400 billion, ranging from $375 billion in losses to the maximum loss appraised at $575 billion per annum. Losses due to cybersecurity attacks and cybercrimes often have far reaching impact on all people affecting the national income of industrialized and developing countries, private and public organizations and global vulnerable citizens. Data obtained from researchers such as Blair, Huntsman, Jon, Craig, Slade, William, Wince-Smith & Young (2014); Lewis & Baker, (2014); Cashell, Jackson, Jickling & Webel (2014) and McClarkin, (2014) from their studies of 32 countries carried out in June 2014 for the Center for Strategic and International Studies on the economic impact of cybersecurity and cybercrimes on the global economy and the estimated cost of cybercrime are staggering.

Estimated Net Losses Due to Cybersecurity Attacks and Cybercrimes on Global Population

Nations	Net Losses
Australia	(.08%)
Brazil	(.32%)
Canada	(.17%)
China	(.63%)
European Union	(.41%)
France	(.11%)
Germany	(1.60%)
India	(.21%)
Japan	(.02%)
Mexico	(.17%)
Russia	(.10%)
Saudi Arabia	(.17%)
Turkey	(.07%)
United Kingdom	(.16%)
United States	(.64%)
Argentina	(Not Applicable)
Colombia	(.14%)
Indonesia	(Not Applicable)
Ireland	(.20%)
Italy	(.18%)
Kenya	(.01%)
Korea	(Not Applicable)
Malaysia	(.18%)
Netherlands	(1.62%)
New Zealand	(.09%)
Nigeria	(.25%)
Norway	(.64%)
Singapore	(.41%)
South Africa	(.14%)

United Arab Emirate	(.11%)
Vietnam	(.13%)
Zambia	(.19%)

Estimated Net Losses Due to Cybersecurity Attacks on Global Population

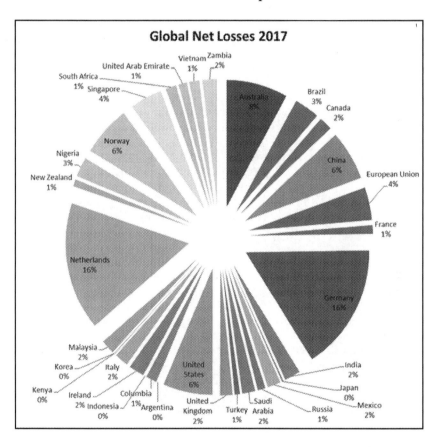

Result of Analysis

As illustrated above, the risk of cybersecurity attacks and cybercriminals is similar and real for either industrial countries and developing countries. The gain and loss indicator is subject to change as low-income countries and affluence nations increase their access point, use of the Internet for commercial purposes and strengthening individual, private and public organization confidence, and trust. All stakeholders must cautiously work with the government and legislators of global populations, under the auspices of the appropriate national security authorities to eradicate cybersecurity threats and cybercrimes.

Cyber Security Threats

Per Cashell, Jackson, Jickling & Webel (2014), the US Department of Homeland Security (DoHS), Departments of Defense (DoD), and Departments of Justice (DoJ) found that except for the Departments of Defense (DoD), most intelligence agencies were not charged with national security and with the responsibility to implement or activate the chain of protective measures against cyber security threats. Per Esin (2016 & 2017), cyber security threat is inevitable, crucial step must be adopted to mitigate volatile threats of impairing fatal effect on global economic operations.

Awareness, Education, and Training

The global higher education enterprise must be prepared and willing to adopt and integrate cybersecurity across the academic curriculum. Cybersecurity attack and cybercrimes do not operate in a vacuum; hence, vulnerable generations must be trained and educated using down-to-earth measures to mitigate cybersecurity attack and cybercrimes. The urgent predicament is the international populations who are struggling with mixed messages, absences of consistent, accurate, and up-to-date information to battle undetected cyber security attacks. Fundamentally, the heart of every occupation, profession and livelihood involves the use of digital technologies, the Internet and Website in all operations.

Consequently, global cyber-security education must be structured to move beyond the current instructional and learning endeavors. Cybersecurity is a commanding and promising discipline for citizens and communities of the world because there is practically zero unemployment among cybersecurity professions, and the global demand will outpace supply of cybersecurity professionals at every level in the next seven years.

There is indeed an urgent need for the higher education system to integrate cybersecurity across academic subject areas, and to employ and assign cybersecurity architects and experienced personnel to facilitate security education process. The prime purpose of cybersecurity education (CE) is to prepare the new generation on the integration of work defense so that they are equipped to protect the defenseless community against culprits. Cybersecurity researchers such as Esin (2017), Smith (2015), Givens (2015), LeClair and Keeley (2015) cited weaknesses in intelligence collaboration and sharing, shortage of cybersecurity expert to help in crime scene investigation and data analysis and support worldwide economic setback and provide financially viable collaboration amongst developed and developing nations. Cybersecurity academic program must include standard degree requirements and more course offerings on cybersecurity.

The process must operate without non-judgmental, non-directional, non-intimidating and my-way or no-way academic prerogative department approach. Students, regardless of academic disciple, gender, age, or ethnicity must be mandated to successfully complete two courses in cybersecurity to fulfil the degree requirement to guarantee expansion of global professionals in cybersecurity. Integration of cybersecurity course offerings across the curriculum will help to implement aggressive measures to battle cybersecurity threats and cybercriminals, eradicate cyber espionage and undercover activities threatening innocent human population. As Lewis & Baker (2014) and Castaldo (2015) noted, cybersecurity threats, cyber espionage and cybercriminals are a punitive high-level operation affecting private and public organizations and higher education institutions and must be eradicated through effective instructional and learning endeavors.

Cybersecurity threats are not a city, local, states and national setbacks or predicaments; they are conventional and bound to happen nationally and internationally. The world community must, in one voice, denounce cybersecurity threats, cyber espionage and cybercriminal and support the determined efforts of educational systems to prepare the new generation for impending global danger and war on hacking, cyberterrorism, eavesdropping, espionage and spying on individuals, organizations and countries. These criminals use illegal and unauthorized techniques to extract valuable secrets which threaten the security of global economies, organizations and the world community. Institutional academic curricula must involve all-embracing lecture sessions, training, workshops and conferences, creation of multidimensional lines of action, polygonal, reliable, tenable communications, information intelligent sharing, human collaboration, privacy, respect for lives, protection and the right to self-defense. Upon completion, graduates will be quite prepared and equipped to protect and defend callous perpetrators of cybersecurity threats against private and public organizations and the global economy.

Downside of Multidimensional Approach against Cybersecurity Threats

Per Blair, Huntsman, Jon, Craig, Slade, William, Wince-Smith & Young (2014), Lewis & Baker (2014), and Fitzgerald and Schneider (2015), a multidimensional line of action represents the best approach to battle unsympathetic high-level urbane cybercriminals. The point of reference was exemplified on the initial strategy to battle cybercrime by using the widely publicized Budapest Cybercrime Convention (BCC) approach which, unfortunately, was viewed as ineffective. BCC was the first international treaty seeking to battle the Internet cybersecurity threats and cybercrimes. The BCC stratagem was to synchronize national laws, improve investigation techniques and amplify collaboration amongst nations. The BCC treaty was established by the council of Europe in Strasbourg, France with active participation of the Council of Europe with Canada, Japan, South Africa and the United States as observer states. The BCC explanatory report was written, synthesized and adopted by the Committee of Ministers of the Council of Europe at the 109th session on November 8, 2001.It was ready for signature in Budapest on November 23, 2001 and promulgated into operation in July 2004. Furthermore, McClain (2014) and Blair et al (2014) revealed that ten (10) years after the adoption of BCC report, forty-nine (49) out of one hundred and ninety (190) nations worldwide ratified the convention report in March 2016. Six other states singed the convention report, but did ratified. Brazil and India declined to sign the convention report, while Russia vehemently opposed the entire convention report. BCC was designed as a mandatory international binding instrument against cybersecurity threats. In spite of its distinction and notoriety, it was widely agreed that the Budapest Cybercrime Convention was ineffective (Blair, Huntsman, Jon, Craig, Slade, William, Wince-Smith & Young, (2014); Lewis & Baker, (2014 and Fitzgerald & Schneider, 2015). Multidimensional discrepancy led to the failure of the first international treaty seeking to battle the Internet cybersecurity threats and cybercrimes. This failure to unite in this fight against global terrorism and cyber threats inadvertently promoted and widened the horizon of cybersecurity threats, cyber espionage against private and public organizations and higher education institutions and the global economy.

Chapter 4-B: Professional Engagement

Per Esin (2017), Chapple and Seidi (2016), Harris and Ham (2016), McMillan and Abernathy (2014), and Harris (2008), strengthening of instruction and learning process must be reinforced through professional engagement.

Phase I

1. You have been retained as IT director, based on the current technology evolution. Do you plan to retain cloud technology for securing of the organization's data and information and why?

2. Discuss advantages and disadvantages of the Budapest Cybercrime Convention (BCC), the first international treaty seeking to battle the Internet cybersecurity threats and cybercrimes on private and public organizations and higher education institutions and global economy.

Phase II

3. The use of encryption process to ensure the confidentiality privacy and security of information is known as.

    a. Integrity
    b. Interoperability
    c. Authorization
    d. Availability

4. Which privacy and security problem is impacting healthcare organizations adopting cloud technology without official authorization to users?

    a. Private shareholders
    b. Increased storage
    c. Multitenant environment

    d. Law enforcement

5. You have been hired as Information technology (IT) director for Alpha organization and your counterparts are using Internet-delivered inventory, storage and backup solutions from independent providers. What type of cloud technology will be appropriate for your operation?

    a. Private cloud technology
    b. Public cloud technology
    c. Community cloud technology
    d. Retail cloud technology

6. Purchasing software and providing and engaging a third party to install, configure and manage the program is an example of the following:

    a. Virtualization service provider
    b. Platform as a service
    c. Public cloud technology
    d. Application service provider

7. You have been retained as a software developer for Abrams Organization and you decided to build and test your Web application in a cloud facility. Identify the type of cloud technology that is appropriate for the operation.

    a. PaaS
    b. SaaS
    c. IaaS
    d. XaaS

8. Which of the following is considered a cloud client?

    a. Router device
    b. Operation
    c. Web browser

d. V-LAN

9. A scaled-down client computer that connects to a hosted resource instead of running the resources locally is known as

   a. Virtual machine
   b. Thin client
   c. Super computer
   d. Thick client

10. An organization that delivers cloud services is known as

    a. Locally hosted entity
    b. Cloud service alliance
    c. Cloud service provider
    d. Community cloud

11. Organizations have decided that they will no longer want to maintain their file server and network environment because of increasing costs and liability. The organizations want to move to a cloud-based technology solution, but need to determine which type of technology solution that will best fit the organization's needs. To the best of your knowledge, which of the following provides the correct definition and mapping of a typical cloud-based technology solutions?

    i. Software as a Service is provided when a cloud provider delivers a software environment in the form of a computer platform.
    ii. Platform as a Service is provided when a cloud provider delivers a computing platform that can include operating system, database and Web server.
    iii. Software as a Service is provided when a cloud provider delivers an infrastructure environment like a traditional data center
    iv. Infrastructure as a Service is provided when a cloud technology provider delivers a computing platform that includes operating system, database and Web servers.

12. Alpha organization is considering the use of an object based storage system where data and information are placed in a provider-managed storage environment using application programming interface (API) calls. What type of cloud technology to service is appropriate for the operations?

    a. IaaS
    b. PaaS
    c. CaaS
    d. SaaS
    e. Which of these items clearly describes the impact of a data breach?
    a. Host system malfunction
    b. Increase of patient data and information
    c. Withholding of medical history
    d. Unauthorized disclosure of patient information

13. In what model of cloud technology can two or more organizations collaborate to build a shared cloud computing environment designed to accommodate the two entities?

    a. Public cloud technology
    b. Network cloud technology
    c. Community cloud technology
    d. Private cloud technology

14. Identify the type of exploited vulnerability allowing more input than the program that has allocated space to store organization data and information.

    a. Symbolic links
    b. File description
    c. Buffer overflows
    d. Kernel flaws

15. Identify which one of these safeguard tools can be used to create privacy issues involving collecting secrete data and information on users.

    a. Malware forensic
    b. Chief information officer
    c. Medical device manufacturer
    d. Indemnification

16. Joseph is carrying out a software analysis on his organization's proprietary application. He has found out that it is possible for attackers to force an authorization step to take place before the authentication step is completed successfully. What is the appropriate measure that will not allow compromise to take place?

    a. Back door
    b. Data validation error
    c. Race condition
    d. Maintenance hook

17. Identify a typical deployment model allowing cloud technology to be accessed by groups of similar or identical organizations.

    a. Public cloud
    b. Private cloud
    c. Community cloud
    d. Hybrid cloud

18. Which of the following Malware virus entrenched and build-in propagation mechanism that exploit system vulnerability to spread into organization network system?

    a. Trojan horse
    b. Worm
    c. Logic bomb
    d. Hacking

19. Identify an organization's greatest concern about cloud storage technology:

    a. Availability
    b. Security
    c. Elasticity
    d. Redundancy

20. The modern cloud-technology access involves connection application programs, resources and services at which of the following?

    a. Local area network
    b. Through a VPN
    c. WAN connection
    d. Across the Internet
    e. PAN network

21. Maurice plans to send Felicia a message with the confidence that recipient will know the message will not be altered while in transit. Identify the objective of cryptography Maurice is trying accomplished.

    a. Confidentiality
    b. Nonrepudiation
    c. Authentication
    d. Integrity

22. Which one of the following is a mixture of a public and a private cloud?

    a. Home cloud technology
    b. Infrastructure technology
    c. Hybrid cloud technology
    d. WAN-cloud technology

23. What cloud computing technology will organizations adopt to build a cloud computing environment in their own data facilities for official users?(

    a. Public cloud
    b. Community cloud
    c. Private cloud
    d. Shared cloud

24. Cloud-based technology used to provide account provision, administration, management, authentication, authorization, reporting and monitoring capabilities is listed as what type of cloud service?

    a. PaaS
    b. DaaS
    c. IaaS
    d. SaaS

25. The availability of authentication is the biggest organization's priority. What type of identity platform should be recommended for operation?

    a. Outsource
    b. Cloud computing
    c. Hybrid computing
    d. Mission computing

26. If an organization's IT Director needs to share identity information with a counterpart, what should the director scrutinize?

    a. Single sign-on
    b. Multidimensional
    c. Federation
    d. DaaS

27. Identify which one of the following does not occur in a single sign-on implementation.

    a. ADES encryption
    b. CAS encryption
    c. Kerberos
    d. RAC encryption

28. Which of the following is not a type of attack used against access control?

    a. Tunnel attacks
    b. Dictionary attack
    c. Brute force attack
    d. Authentication attack

29. As a subject is claiming an identity, what process is transpiring?

    a. Login on system
    b. Identification
    c. Authentication
    d. Confidentiality

30. Body guards, wire fences and door keys are common examples of what types of access control?

    a. Detective operation
    b. Physical operation
    c. Identification operation
    d. Tech-support operation

31. The store sample of biometric factor is known as

    a. Enrollment artifact
    b. Reference template
    c. Biometric password
    d. Fingerprint search

32. During a penetration text, Theresa recovers a file containing hashed passwords she is attempting to access. What type of attack is most likely to succeed against the hashed password?

    a. A brute force attacks
    b. A pass-the-has attack
    c. A rainbow table attack
    d. A salt recovery attack

33. The X.500 standards cover what type of important identity system?

    a. Kerberos Services
    b. Biometric Services
    c. Provision services
    d. Directory services

Review Question Answers

1. A
2. A
3. C
4. D
5. A
6. C
7. B
8. C
9. B
10. A
11. D
12. C
13. C
14. B
15. B
16. B
17. C
18. B
19. B
20. D
21. C
22. C
23. C
24. C
25. C
26. C
27. C
28. B
29. B
30. B
31. B
32. C
33. D

CHAPTER 5

Fundamentals of Cryptography

Cryptography is derived from the Greek *KRYPTOS,* meaning hidden. The origin of cryptography is usually dated from about 2000 BC, with the Egyptian practice of hieroglyphics and consisted of complex pictograms with the full meaning known to few elite. As McMillan and Abernathy (2014) and Stallings (2015) posited, the first known use of a modern cipher was by Julius Caesar (100 BC to 44 BC), who did not trust his messengers when communicating with his governors and officers and for this reason, he created a system in which each character in his messages was replaced by a character three positions ahead of it in the Roman alphabet. In recent times, cryptography has turned into a battleground of some of the world's best mathematicians and computer scientists with ability to securely store and transfer sensitive information. Most of this hiding was particularly important and necessary during the Cold War era and in today's cyber warfare when the slightest information can determine the fate of the world.

Most global governments do not want certain entities to have access and means to receive and send hidden information that can threaten the national interests. As a result, cryptography has been subject to various restrictions in most countries, ranging from limitations of the usage to the export of software (McMillan and Abernathy, 2014). However, the Internet has allowed the spread of powerful programs, precisely, the underlying techniques of cryptography. Today, most advanced cryptosystems and ideas are now in the public domain, but cryptography is still the art of writing statue of privacy, the secret method of coding of data and information back to 500 to 600 BC (McMillan & Abernathy, 2014; and Stallings, 2015).

The evolution of human civilizations witnessed the reorganizing of most entities into tribes, villages, cities, states, kingdoms and nations. The emergence of human redeployment invigorated the natural need for populace to establish secret codes of communication with selective inheritors which in turn guaranteed the continuous evolution of cryptography. The myth of cryptography includes cryptosystems, outmoded and modern-day ciphers, public key encryption, data integration, message authentication, and digital signatures. Cryptography is one of the original cultures of Roman and Egyptian civilizations of 4000 years ago, where Egyptian traditional writing involved the use hieroglyph to transmit and communicate secret manages to leaders and citizens. Hieroglyph is the oldest cryptographic secrets code used by the scribes to transmit messages on behalf of kings, suzerains and royals. Modern scholars adopted simple mono-alphabetic substitution ciphers during 500 to 600 BC to replace alphabets of message with alternative alphabets of secret language, rule and keys (McMillan and Abernathy, 2014). The prevailing rule turned into a key to retrieve the message back from the confused secret message. The earlier Roman modus of cryptography, popularly known as the **Caesar Shift Cipher**, relies on shifting the letters of a message by an agreed number (three was a common choice), the recipient of this message would then shift the letters back by the same number and obtain the original message.

Per McMillan and Abernathy (2014) and Shinder and Tittel (2002), cryptography is a thought-provoking chronicle, which continues to undergo challenges. It has played a very significant role in history of human civilization and the modern study of cryptography is credited with expanding individuals' and organization's ability to hide true intentions in order to gain competitive edges and reduce human vulnerabilities due to advances in technology. Cryptography-technology has incorporated streams of binary code that pass over network wires, Internet communication channels and airwaves.

Cryptography + Security + Encryption = hexing

Substitution Cipher ➡ Monoalphabetic ➡ Polyalphabetic ➡ Multiple Alphabets

Per McMillan and Abernathy (2014) and Harris (2008), substitution cipher known as monoalphabetic entrenched with one alphabet was replaced with polyphasers with multiple alphabets. In about 400 B. C. the Spartans used a system of encrypting data and information to write messages on papyrus wrapped around wooden rod to deliver information to recipients. The messages were readable if they were wrapped with the correct and matching size of wooden rod. In about 100 B.C. in Rome, Julius Caesar developed a simple method of shifting letters of the alphabets like a bash scheme and shifted the alphabets by three positions. The shifted alphabet is known as algorithm and the key is the number of locations shifted during the encryption and decryption operations.

Traditional Alphabet:	ABCDEFGHIJK<u>L</u>MN<u>O</u>PQ<u>R</u>STUVWXYZ
Cryptographic Alphabet:	DEFGHIJK<u>L</u>MN<u>O</u>PQ<u>R</u>STUVWXYZABC

As posted above, encryption algorithm process involves taking the first letter of the message; L and shifting up three locations within the alphabet. The encryption algorithm will involve moving letter O to match letter R that is shifted three places. Upon successful completion of the encryption algorithm process, a carrier will take modern encryption version to the destination that will eventually lead to a reversed process. Per Harris (2008), cryptography increased and restored confidence insecurity operation for over three decades and strengthened individuals' and organizations' cryptography.

Access control – act of controlling and restricting subject and object access operation.

Algorithm – set of mathematical rules used in encryption and decryption activities.

Cipher – common name for algorithm

Cryptography – science of secrete writing allowing organizations to store and transmit data and information in a form available to for the intended recipient.

Cryptosystem – process of implementing hardware and software cryptography that transforms a message to cipher text and back to plaintext.

Cryptanalysis – practice of breaking cryptic system to decipher messages

Cryptology – a study of cryptography and cryptanalysis

Data Origin Authentication – authentic sources of a message

Encipher – act of transforming data and information into an unreadable format

Entity Authentication - proven identity of the entity that sent a message

Decipher – act of transforming data into a readable format

Key – secret sequence of bits and instructions that governing the act of encryption and decryption.

Key Clustering – activities when two different keys generate the same ciphertext from the same plaintext.

Key space – range of possible values used to construct keys

Plaintext – data and information in readable format known as cleartext

Receipt – acknowledgment of message that has been received

Work Factor – estimated time, effort and resources require to break cryptosystem.

Steganography - an added component of cryptography used to protect the secrecy of data and information against unauthorized users through watermarking or alternative measures. In steganography, perpetrators and interlopers are unaware that observed data and messages contain hidden information; whereas, in cryptography, perpetrators and intruders are often aware of the data and information in progress and can understand the coded and scrambled message. During the European Renaissance, several Italian and Papal states adopted the proliferation of cryptographic techniques and the adopted measures which led to unveiling and breaking data and information secrets codes.

Cumulatively, the break through led to the discovery of compatible codes techniques the Vigenere Coding in the 15th century, which offered moving letters in the message with several variable places instead of moving them within the same number of places. Additional changes occurred in the 19th century when cryptography evolved from the informal approaches to encryption and sophisticated art of science of information security. Thereafter, there was the invention of mechanical and electromechanical machines, such as the Enigma rotor machine with advanced and efficient means of coding data and information in the early 20th century (McMillan & Abernathy, 2014).

During the Second World War, **cryptography** and **cryptanalysis** turned out to be a mathematical operation and was adopted by the military units and government agencies who used the technique to protect their secret operations. Cryptography is the cornerstone of computer and communications security and the mathematical system such as number theory, computational-complexity theory, and probability theory. Cryptography is categorized into three classifications: cryptology, cryptosystems and cryptanalysis (McMillan & Abernathy, 2014; and Stallings, 2015).

Cryptography – Cryptography is the art and science of making a cryptosystem for information security. It is a science involving securing of digital data and mechanisms of mathematical algorithms used to provide fundamental information for security services and the establishment of a large toolkit containing different techniques for security applications.

Cryptanalysis -A branch of cryptography, cryptoanalysis is the art and science of breaking the cipher text often in the use cipher text for transmission and storage and to test security strengths.

Cryptosystem - a suite of cryptographic algorithms designed to implement a security service, most commonly for achieving confidentiality (encryption) and consists of three algorithms: one for key generation, one for encryption, and one for decryption. The philosophy of cryptography is to provide data and information security. Four fundamental data and information security services reinforcing the projected objectives of cryptography include confidentiality, data integrity, authentication and non-repudiation.

Confidentiality - the fundamental security service provided by cryptography to protect data and information from unauthorized users otherwise known as privacy or secrecy. This credible means involves the use of physical and mathematical algorithms and encryptions of data, information and languages.

Data Integrity - a security service that deals with identifying any alteration to the data. The data may get modified by an unauthorized entity intentionally or accidently. Integrity service confirms whether data is intact or not since it was last created, transmitted, or stored by an authorized user. Data integrity cannot prevent the alteration of data, but provides a means for detecting whether data has been manipulated in an unauthorized manner. Per Shinder and Tittel (2002), data integrity in the context of cryptography attest to mean and to verify that data and information was not altered and modified prior to leaving the host system to the recipient system.

Authentication - provides the identification of the originator to confirm to the recipient that data and information sent is legitimate, authentic and verified by the sender. Authentication service has two variants— message authentication identifying the originator of the message without regard to the sending router or the system and entity authentication assuring that data and information are received by the recipient.

Authorization – process of providing an identity with user name and password to access the system without authorization. Authorization is the function of specifying access rights to resources related to information security and computer security and direct access control into the system. An organization's fiscal affairs unit often authorizes payroll officers access to records, policy and formalized procedures to the organization's computer network system and complete authorization with ability to decide whose employees should be granted or rejected authorization to organization payroll system.

Non-repudiation - a security service ensuring the original creator of the data and information cannot deny the ownership of the creation and transmission and ignore previous commitment of data and information sent to a recipient. In addition, non-repudiation occurs when the author of a statement or document cannot challenge the authorship. Such situation a is often seen in a legal setting wherein the authenticity of a signature is being challenged or repudiated.

Cryptography includes techniques such as microdots or merging words with images to hide information in storage. Today in a computer-centric world, cryptography is most often associated with scrambling plaintext known as ordinary text, cleartext, ciphertext and encryption. Professional who practice this field are known as cryptographers and protocols that meet these criteria are known as cryptosystems. Cryptosystems are often related to mathematical procedures and computer programs; however, these procedures are involved in the regulation of human behavior, such as choosing hard-to-guess passwords, logging off unused systems, and not discussing sensitive procedures with strangers and interlopers. Cryptography is a set of primitive codes of data, information, messages and languages selectively used to protect security services including, encryption, hash functions, message authentication codes (MAC) and digital signatures. Per Shinder and Tittel (2002) Stallings (2015), cryptographic is often integrated into a security service's system known as cryptosystem. A cryptosystem is a representation of cryptographic techniques designed to provide information security services and can be identified as a **cipher system**. Cryptosystem provides confidentiality to data and information from the sender to the recipient.

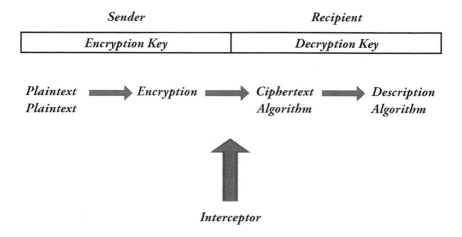

Upon completion of data and information transmission through the cryptosystem from sender to receiver, the two parties involved in the process (sender and receiver) will be able to identify the plaintext. Eight components of cryptosystem include encryption key, decryption key, encryption algorithm, plaintext-sender, ciphertext, decryption algorithm, plaintext-recipient and interceptor.

Plaintext - protected data and information transmitted in its original format and identified as cleartext.

Encryption Algorithm - A mathematical process designed to produce ciphertext for plaintext and encryption key.

Ciphertext - A plaintext produced through the encryption algorithm by means of encryption key, **ciphertext** is not guarded and flows on public channels and can be intercepted by users who have access to the communication channel.

Decryption Algorithm – It is a mathematical process designed to produce a unique plaintext for ciphertext and decryption key; it is a cryptographic algorithm that takes a ciphertext and a decryption key as input and outputs of a plaintext.

Joseph O. Esin

Encryption Key - A value that is known to the sender. The sender inputs the encryption key into the encryption algorithm with the plaintext to compute the ciphertext.

Decryption Key - A value that is clearly known to the receiver. The decryption key is related to the encryption key, but not identical. The receiver often inputs the decryption key into the decryption algorithm with the cyphertext to compute the plaintext. A collection of decryption keys is called a **Key Space**.

Interceptor (attacker) is an unauthorized user with the determination to control the plaintext. The perpetrators can get the drift of the cyphertext, know the decryption algorithm but cannot control the decryption key.

Symmetric Key Encryption - Encryption processes use the same keys for encrypting and decrypting of information known as Symmetric Key Encryption. Symmetric cryptosystem is often referred to as the secret key of cryptosystems. Most symmetric key encryptions comprise of Digital Encryption Standard (DES), Triple-DES (3DES), IDEA, and BLOWFISH. Cryptosystems are a byproduct of encryption-decryption traditionally known as Symmetric Key Encryption (SKE) whereas, Asymmetric Key Encryption (AKE) is end-product of encryption and decryption keys.

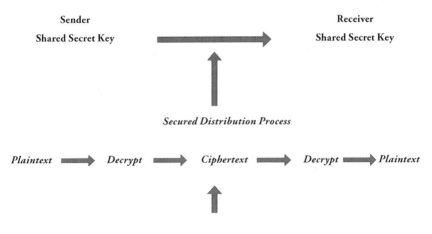

Per McMillan and Abernathy (2014), the use of cryptosystem on symmetric key encryption can be illustrated as follows: Felicia using symmetric key encryption must be willing to share a common key prior to exchange of data and information. These Keys are designed to be changed regularly to prevent any attack on the system. A robust mechanism needs to exist to exchange the key between the communicating parties. Furthermore, keys are required to be changed on a regular basis, though such mechanisms are very expensive. In Felicia (F)'s group, to enable two-party communication between any two individuals, the number of keys required for group is **n × (n − 1)/2**. Per Shinder and Tittel (2002), challenges for using symmetric key cryptography involves the use of one key. A system user needs a pair of dissimilar keys, private key and public key, and these keys are mathematically related. If Key-A is used for encrypting the data, Key-B is used to decrypt the ciphertext back to the original plaintext. The process requires placing the public key in public repository and the private key in a well-guarded secret key-holder. This chain ends in the scheme of encryption known as Public Key Encryption.

The strength of the well-guarded secret scheme reveals that the public and private keys of the system users are interrelated, but not computationally feasible to uncover public key from private key. When Maurice (M-1) is ready to send data to Felicia (F-2); M-1 will obtain the public key of F-2 storehouse, encrypt the data and transmit. F-2, the recipient will use the Private Key to extract the plaintext. The length of public and private keys is measured in the number of bits and the encryption is large; consequently, the process of encryption-decryption through asymmetric key encryption is slower than symmetric key encryption. The processing power of computer system required to run asymmetric algorithm is higher than the processing of computer power to run symmetric algorithm. The Challenge of Public Key Cryptosystem (CPKC) has one notable encounter allowing M-1the sender to trust the public key used in transmitting the data to F-1who has a public key that has not been spoofed by a spiteful third party.

Public Key Infrastructure (PKI) involves a trusted third party and the noted third party is designed to secure, manage and attest to the authenticity of public keys. As McMillan and Abernathy (2014) maintain that when the third-party M-1 is requested to provide the public key for any communicating to F-1, they are trusted to provide the correct public key for each other. The third party satisfies itself about user identity by the process of verification and authentication process indicating that M-1 has the only one unique key. The most conjoint method to authenticate public keys is entrenchment in a certificate of authentication which is digitally authorized by the trusted third party. Public Key Infrastructure (PKI) contains the certificate storage facilities of a certificate server and provides certificate management facilities including the ability to issue, revoke, store, retrieve, and trust certificates. The focal feature of a PKI is the introduction of a certification authority *(CA)*, such as entity, individual, group, department, segment of an organization authorized to issue certificates to users. CA creates certificates and digitally authorizes its use as private key and becomes the principal component of a PKI. The formats of digital certificate are a collection of categorizing information bound together with a public key and authorized by a trusted third party to prove its authenticity. A digital certificate can be one of several different formats. Pritty-good privacy (PGP) provides e-mail encryption over the Internet and uses different encryption technologies needed by organizations and able to support confidentiality, integrity and authentication for encryption process. The process recognizes two types of formats PGP certificates and X.509 certificates (McMillan & Abernathy, 2014).

PGP version number - used to create keys related to **certificate holder's public key (CHPK), is a version of** public key paired together with the algorithm of other keys such as **Ron Rivets, Adi Shamir and Leonard Adelman** (RSA), Diffie-Hellman (DH) and Digital Signature Algorithm (DSA).

Digital signature of the certificate owner – known as self-signature, must correspond with private key and public key associated with the certificate. Certificate's start and expiration date and time must be clearly indicated to ensure the certificate's validity period.

Symmetric encryption algorithm - encrypted information assigned to certificate owners and supported algorithms include Carlisle Adams and Stafford Tavares (CAST), International Data Encryption Algorithm

(IDEA) and Digital Encryption Standard (DES) and Triple Digital Encryption Standard (3DES).

X. 509 Certificate Format - *X.509* is a common certificate format often operated in compliance with ITU-T X.509 international standard and upon creation; it can apply to different applications. However, most organizations have created compatible X.509 certificates that strongly require users to validate their specific public key and name of the key's owner. Creation of PGP certificates allows users to validate their identity whereas X.509 certificates designate validator as Certification Authority not a user. X.509 certificate is a collection of a standard set of fields containing information users, device and corresponding public key.

Digital Certificates

Digital Certificate (DC) is the process of providing authorized entity for a user and credentials used to prove that such identity is associated with a public key. Digital certification must specify essential items such as serial number, issuer, authorized user (owner) and the public key and confirmation that the DC is genuine and valid. An authorized digital certificate must be entrenched with three critical items such as public key a certificate of identity of the user including unique user name, a private password and authentic digital signatures. As McMillan and Abernathy (2014) posit, in the nineteenth century, a Dutch cryptographer Auguste Kirchhoff developed six systematic principles for the military use of ciphers. These six guiding principles for the military use of ciphers are as follows:

* System must be practical, mathematical and indecipherable;
* System must be required to be secret and must not be able to fall into the hands of the enemy without inconvenience;
* System must be communicable and retainable without the help of written notes, changeable and modifiable at the will of the correspondence;
* System must be applicable to telegraphic correspondence;
* System must be portable, and its usage and function must not require the concourse of several people; and

* System must be easy to use, requiring neither mental strain nor the knowledge of a long series of rules to observe.

Kirchhoff's guiding principles are directly related to cryptosystem that must be unbreakable and practically without mathematical function. Per McMillan and Abernathy (2014), Kirchhoff's principles are often applied in encryption algorithms by digital encryption standard (DES) and advanced encryption standard (AES) and these public algorithms must be kept under tight security. Cryptography must in one way or the other be connected to the Internet; hence, Kirchhoff's principles are essential guidelines for designing algorithms in cutting-edge cryptography. Validation of Trust in cryptography is imperative since every user in a public key system is vulnerable to mistaking a fake certificate for a real one. The principles therefore reinforce that established public key certificate is authentic and belongs to its authorized owner. Authentication is an important instrument to support a public key environment ensuring that the certificate is original and genuine. In an organization using a PKI with X.509 certificates, it is the responsibility of the CA to issue authentic certificates to users that often requires responding to a user's request for original certificate. Stallings (2015) noted that the alternative step to check user's public key for validity is going through manual process whereby recipients physically receive a copy of the public key. The procedure is often inconvenient and inefficient because it requires the manual checking of the certificate owner's fingerprint. Authority (root CA) and is a trusted introducer subordinate Certification Authorities. The trust model creates pathways for users to validate certificate authority and there are three atypical models: Direct Trust, Hierarchical Trust, and A Web of Trust.

Maurice	←——————→	Felicia
(User-1)		(User-2)

Assumptions of Attacker

Cryptosystem Environment is entrenched with two categories of attacks known as cryptography algorithms: public algorithms and proprietary algorithms. Proprietary algorithms security is often ensured through obscurity and private algorithms is apparently the strongest algorithms, but weak. Private algorithms developed in-house permit communication among closed groups and considered not suitable for communication with large groups or large segments of known or unknown entities. The assumption of security environment is the encryption algorithm known as **the attacker**.

In the process, an attacker can falsely accept that there is a direct access to the ciphertext generated through the cryptosystem. Once the attacker can determine the key, the targeted system is considered as not a working system. Methodologies used to attack cryptosystems are categorized as follows:

Ciphertext Only Attacks (COA) - attackers can have access to a set of ciphertexts not plaintext and COA is effective when plaintext is controlled by a set of ciphertexts.

Known Plaintext Attack (KPA) - attackers have identified plaintext from ciphertext and major task is how to decrypt most portions of ciphertext and the best approach to combat such attack is through linear cryptanalysis against block ciphers.

Chosen Plaintext Attack (CPA) – attackers now have **the** choice of encrypted text and ciphertext-plaintext pair of text. An example of this attack is differential cryptanalysis applied against block ciphers as well as hash functions.

Dictionary Attack - attackers have most variants, all of which involve compiling a dictionary. The simplest method of this attack is that an attacker builds a dictionary of ciphertext and corresponding plaintexts that he has learnt over a period. In future, when an attacker gets the ciphertext, he refers to the dictionary to find the corresponding plaintext.

Brute Force Attack (BFA) - attackers try to determine the key by attempting all possible keys. If the key is 8 bits long, then the number of possible keys is 2^8 = 256. The attacker knows the ciphertext and the algorithm, now he attempts all the 256 keys one by one for decryption. The time to complete the attack would be very long if the key is long.

Birthday Attack – attackers have various kinds of brute-force technique to use against the cryptographic hash function. When Maurice is asked about her birthday, the answer was one of the possible 365 dates. Apparently, Maurice's birthdate is 3rd Aug and Felicia's is 3rd Aug. There is a need to enquire $1.25 * \sqrt{365} \approx 25$ for Maurice and Felicia. Equally, if the hash function produces 64-bits hash values, the possible hash values are 1.8×10^{19}. By repeatedly evaluating the function for different inputs, the same output is expected to be obtained after about 5.1×10^9 random inputs. If the attacker can find two different inputs that give the same hash value, it is a collision and that hash function is said to be broken.

Man in Middle Attack (MIMA) - targets of such attacks are mostly public key cryptosystems where key exchange is involved before communication takes place. When Maurice (a Host-A) is ready to send communicate to Felicia (a Host -B), a public key of *B* will be requested. If attackers intercept the request and send his public key instead, to maintain communication, the attacker re-encrypts the data after reading with his public key and sends to *B*. The attacker sends his public key as *A*'s public key so that *B* takes it as if it is taking it from *A*.

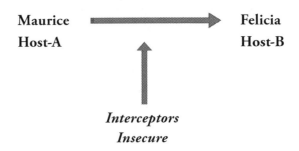

Side Channel Attack (SCA) – The attacker is not against cryptosystem or algorithm, but is willing to exploit weaknesses in the physical implementation of the cryptosystem.

Timing Attacks (TA) – attackers exploit the fact that computations take much time to compute on processor, and measuring such timings reveals that it is possible to know about a computation on processor and encryption.

Power Analysis Attacks (PAA) – attackers realize actual amount of power consumption used to obtain information about the nature of the underlying computations.

Elliptic-Curve Cryptosystems (ECC) - Per McMillan and Abernathy (2014), a ECC provides secure key distribution, encryption and digital signature. Advantages of elliptic-curve include encryption scheme that is highly attractive for application where computing resources are stored including symmetric private key and asymmetric public key schemes used to achieve the confidentiality and integrity of data and information. The two diverse types of data integrity threats include passive integrity and active integrity threats.

Passive Integrity Threats (PIT) - PIT exists as a result of accidental variations or errors in system data and information and the data errors often occur due to noise in a communication channel. In the process system data, an information is likely to be corrupted while data files are stored on storage devices. Error-correcting codes and simple checksums such as Cyclic Redundancy Checks (CRCs) are frequently used to detect the loss of data integrity and such an approach leads to a technique known as a digest of data that is computed mathematically and affixed to the data.

Active Integrity Threats (AIT) - occurs as attackers can manipulate the data with malicious intent and if data exist without digest such data can be modified without detection. AIT tend to use methods of appending Cyclic Redundancy Checks (CRC) to data for detecting any active modification. However, on higher level of threats, attackers may modify data and try to derive new digest to modify data from exiting digest. Security mechanisms such as Hash Functions are used to tackle the active integrity threats. Hash Functions are extremely useful and appear in almost all information security applications.

Hash Functions (HF) - Hash function is a mathematical function that converts a numerical input value into compressed numerical value. An input to the hash function is of arbitrary length while output is always of fixed length. Typical features of hash functions include a hash function for an input x which produces hash value h(x); then it should be difficult to find any extra input value y such that h(y) = h(x). This property of hash function protects against an attacker who has an input value and its hash, and wants to substitute a different value as legitimate value in place of original input value.

Collision Resistance (CR) – indicates a byzantine process to locate two diverse inputs of any length resulting in the same hash and such input is also referred to as collision free hash function. As noted by Stalling (2015), a hash function h is hard to find in any two different inputs x and y such that h(x) = h(y). Hash function is compressing function with fixed hash length and it is impossible for a hash function not to have collisions. The property of collision free occurs to confirm that CR is hard to uncover. This property makes it very difficult for an attacker to find two input values with the same hash. Also, if a hash function is collision-resistant then it is also pre-image resistant.

Secure Hash Function (SHA) – The family of SHA comprise of four SHA algorithms namely, SHA-0, SHA-1, SHA-2, and SHA-3. For original SHA-0 version is a 160-bit hash function, published by the National Institute of Standards and Technology (NIST) in 1993. It had few weaknesses and was not very popular. In 1995, SHA-1 was designed to correct alleged weaknesses of SHA-0. SHA-1 is the most widely used of the existing SHA hash functions and employs several widely used applications and protocols including Secure Socket Layer (SSL) security. In 2005, a technique was found for uncovering collisions for SHA-1 within practical time frame making long-term employability of SHA-1 unconvinced.

Secure Hash Function (SHA-2) – This function has four additional SHA variants namely, SHA-224, SHA-256, SHA-384, and SHA-512 depending up on number of bits in their hash value. No successful attacks have been reported on SHA-2 hash function. SHA-2 has a strong hash function. Even though, significantly different, but it can adopt to a basic design structure like SHA-1. In October 2012, the NIST chose the Keccak algorithm as the new SHA-3 standard. Keccak offers many benefits, such as efficient performance and good resistance for attacks.

Message Authentication Code (MAC) - MAC algorithm is a symmetric key cryptographic technique designed to provide message authentication. MAC processes tend to support sender and receiver to share a symmetric key. MAC is an encrypted checksum generated on the underlying message sent along with a message to ensure message authentication. The sender uses MAC algorithm, inputs the message and the secret key to produce a MAC value. A MAC function often compresses an arbitrary long input into a fixed length output. The major difference between hash and MAC is that MAC uses a secret key during the compression. In the process, a sender forwards the message using MAC algorithm with original authentication, not confidentiality, and if confidentiality is involved it will required encryption. Upon receipt of the message from the sender using MAC algorithm, the receiver reviews the message, uses the shared secret key into the MAC algorithm and re-computes the MAC value. The receiver now checks the authenticity or validity of the freshly computed MAC algorithm with the MAC algorithm received from the sender. If there is a match, the receiver accepts the message and assures confirming that the message has been sent by the intended sender (McMillan and Abernathy, 2014).

Importance of Digital Signature (IDS) - digital signature uses public key cryptography with essential tool to achieve information security. IDS have three important fundamental features including non-repudiation of message, message authentication, and data integrity. **Non-repudiation** exists when a user often has the knowledge of the signature key; the sender can create a unique signature using the given data and the receiver can present data and the digital signature to a third party as evidence if any dispute arises in the future.

Message authentication is a process that deals with how to validate the digital signature using a public key from a sender to be assured that the signature was created by an authorized sender in possession of a secret private key.

Data Integrity – It deals with the purity of data and the prevention of an attacker to have access to the data and ability to verify if receiver end fails. By adding public-key encryption to digital signature scheme, we can create a cryptosystem that can provide the four essential elements of security namely: Privacy, Authentication, Integrity, and Non-repudiation (McMillan and Abernathy, 2014; and Stallings 2015).

Chapter 5-B: Professional Engagement

Per Esin (2017), Chapple and Seidi (2016), Harris and Ham (2016), McMillan and Abernathy (2014), and Harris (2008), strengthening of instruction and learning process must be reinforced through professional engagement.

Phase 1

1. When a symmetric key is encrypted with a recipient's public key, what security service is provided?

    Response – the recipient's private key can be used to decrypt the symmetric key and the recipient will now have access to private. **Security service in the process is Confidentiality**

2. When data and information are encrypted with sender's private key, what security is provided?

    Response – recipient can decrypt the encrypted data and information with the sender's public key, because that the data was encrypted with sender's private key. **Security service in the process is Authenticity.**

3. When the sender encrypts data and information with the recipient's private key, what security is provided?

    Response: No security is provided in the process.

4. State the reason why symmetric key is used to encrypt message.

    Response: Symmetric key is fast and asymmetric key is too slow.

Phase II

Instructions: Following the sample answer selection process above, select the letter that best identifies the correct answer to each question:

1. Identify the process that converts a plaintext into a ciphertext.

    a. Hashing
    b. Decryption
    c. Encryption
    d. Digital signature

2. What occurs when different encryption keys generate the same ciphertext from the same plaintext message?

    a. Key clustering
    b. Cryptanalysis
    c. Key space
    d. Cryptography

3. Identify the types of cipher classified as Caesar cipher.

    a. Polyalphabetic substitution
    b. Mono-alphabetic substitution
    c. Polyalphabetic transposition
    d. Trito-alphabetric transportation

4. In cryptography, different steps and algorithms provide dissimilar types of security service. Which of the following provides only authentication, nonrepudiation, and integrity?

    a. Hash algorithm
    b. Encryption algorithm
    c. Digital signature
    d. Encryption paired with a digital signature

5. Which of the following best describes the function of a confidentiality mechanism?

    a. Prevents unauthorized disclosure of data
    b. Prevents data discovery
    c. Prevents unauthorized users from accessing a system with sensitive information

    d. Prevents authorized users from accessing a system with sensitive information

6. What is the name of the machine used by Germany in World War II to encrypt sensitive data?

    a. The Turing Machine
    b. The "Box"
    c. The Enigma Machine
    d. Overclose ln

7. Which of the following best describes Key Derivation Functions (KDF)?

    a. Keys are generated from a master key
    b. Session keys are generated from each other
    c. Asymmetric cryptography is used to encrypt symmetric keys
    d. A master key is generated from a session key

8. What is the purpose of a hash?

    a. A hash provides non-repudiation
    b. A hash provides integrity
    c. A hash provides confidentiality
    d. A hash provides instructions for an algorithm

9. Identify the encryption system that uses a private-secret key that must remain secret between sender and receivers.

    a. Master-symmetric algorithm
    b. Symmetric algorithm
    c. One-time algorithm
    d. Asymmetric algorithm
    e. All the above.

10. An elliptic curve cryptography is an asymmetric algorithm, which segment is the other part of asymmetric algorithm?

    a. More efficient and mathematical structures
    b. Provides digital signatures, secure key distribution and encryption
    c. Computes discrete logarithm in a finite field
    d. Use of larger percentages of resources to carry out encryption

11. Identify which of the following is not a hash function

    a. ECC
    b. MD6
    c. SHA-2
    d. Brute force

12. Identify which attack executed against a cryptographic algorithm uses all possible keys until a key is discovered that successfully decrypts the ciphertext.

    a. Frequency analysis
    b. Reverse engineering
    c. Ciphertext-only attack
    d. Two fish algorithms

13. Identify the objective of cryptography.

    a. To determine the strength of algorithm
    b. To increase the substitution function in a cryptographic algorithm
    c. To decrease the transposition functions in cryptographic algorithm
    d. To deter the permutation

14. Provide logical reason why brute force attacks are increasing across the globe. Due to increased strength on complexity and vulnerability of attacks

    a. Processor speed and power has increased
    b. Key length reduction over-time
    c. Permutation and transpositions in algorithm has increased
    d. Key Processor

15. End-to-end encryption is used by users and link encryption is used by service providers. Which of the following correctly describes the impact of cyber-technology?

    a. Link encryption does not encrypt headers and trailers
    b. Link encryption encrypts everything but data link message
    c. End-to-end encryption requires headers to be decrypted at each hop
    d. End-to-end encryption encrypts all headers and trailers.

16. Advanced Encryption Standard (AES) is an algorithm used for which of the following?

    a. Data integrity
    b. Bulk data encryption
    c. Key recovery
    d. Distribution of symmetric keys

17. Which of the following is a hashing algorithm?

    a. SHA-1
    b. DES
    c. AES
    d. Diffie-Hellman

18. Which of the following protocols blurs the lines between the OSI model layers performing the tasks of several at once?

    a. File transfer protocol (FTP)

    b. Transmission control protocol (TCP)

    c. Distributed network protocol3 (DNP-3)

    d. Domain name system (DNS)

19. What is the purpose of a key?

    a. A key provides the instructions to decrypt encrypted text

    b. A key provides the instructions to encrypt plain text

    c. A key provides math functions to provide encryption or decryption services

    d. A key provides the instructions for an algorithm to encrypt and decrypt data.

20. To ensure authenticity, which key should a sender use?

    a. Their public key

    b. An encrypted password

    c. Their private key

    d. B and C

21. Which function is provided by a virtual private network?

    a. Create a tunnel through the internet

    b. Create a private Wi-Fi signal

    c. Bypass security

    d. None of the above

22. There are several components associated with steganography. dentify which of the following refers to a file that has hidden data and information within a steganography process.

    a. Payload

    b. Fluctuation

    c. Carrier

    d. Enigma

23. Which of the following items best correctly describes a drawback of a symmetric key system?

    a. Carry out mathematically intensive operations
    b. Computationally less intensive than asymmetric systems
    c. The key must be delivered through a secure courier
    d. The key works much more slowly than asymmetric

24. Which key arrangement is required for a symmetric key encryption? Two keys are involved

    a. One key is involved
    b. A and B
    c. None of the above
    d. Two keys is involved

25. Which information should a sender use to ensure confidentiality for the recipient?

    a. The public key and a password
    b. Both the public and private keys
    c. The public key of the recipient
    d. The private key and a password

26. What is the purpose of a VPN concentrator?

    a. Traffic getting to the VPN is concentrated
    b. Traffic getting to the VPN is encrypted
    c. A and B
    d. Traffic getting to the VPN is available

27. How are keys handled with asymmetric encryption?

    a. Two keys are involved
    b. Two identical keys are involved
    c. One odd key is used
    d. None of the above

28. Which function is provided by a virtual private network?

    a. Create a tunnel through the internet
    b. Create a private Wi-Fi signal
    c. Bypass security
    d. None of the above

29. Which characteristic of block ciphers is correct?

    a. Odd or even
    b. 56-bit blocks or 128-bit blocks
    c. 65-bit blocks or 150-bit blocks
    d. On or off

30. Which of the following occurs in a public key infrastructure (PKI) environment?

    a. Registration authority (RA) creates the certificate and certificates authority (CA).
    b. The CA signs the certificates
    c. The RA signs the certificate
    d. The user signs the certificates

31. Which type of data maintains confidentiality when using transport encryption?

    a. A and B
    b. Blocks in motion
    c. Bits in motion
    d. Data in motion

32. If cipher uses a block size of 4, how would data be encrypted?

    a. 4 blocks at a time
    b. 4 bits at a time
    c. 4 characters at a time
    d. 2 bocks consisting of 2 bits each

33. Which of the following correctly describes the differences between public key cryptography (PKC) and public key infrastructure (PKI)?

    a. The PKC is the act of using asymmetric algorithm, while PKI is the act of using a symmetric algorithm
    b. The PKC is used to create public and private key pairs and PKI to perform key exchange and agreement
    c. The PKC provides authentication and nonrepudiation, while PKI provides confidentiality and integrity
    d. The PKC is an alternative name for asymmetric cryptography, while PKI consists of public key cryptography mechanism

34. Choose the type of information encrypted by a stream cipher.

    a. Individually or in bits
    b. As a stream file
    c. In a constant stream
    d. As even blocks

35. Which of the following is the United States federal government's algorithm developed for creating secure message digest?

    a. Data encryption algorithm
    b. Digital signature standard
    c. Secure hash algorithm
    d. Data signature algorithm

36. Veronica needs to calculate how many keys that must be generated for the 260 clients using organization's PKI asymmetric algorithm, how many keys are required?

    a. 33,670
    b. 520
    c. 67,340
    d. 260

37. What is the indication that a message has been modified and changed?

    a. The public key has been altered
    b. The private key has been altered
    c. The message digest has been altered
    d. The message has been encrypted properly

38. What is the advantage of RSA over the DSA?

    a. It provides digital signature and encryption functionality
    b. It uses fewer resources and encrypt faster because it uses symmetric keys
    c. It is a block cipher rather than a stream cipher
    d. It employs a one-time encryption pad

39. Most countries place restriction on the use of encryption cryptography system. Identify the reason for such restriction.

    a. The system can be used against residents
    b. Law enforcement can have misinterpreted the system
    c. Cybercriminals can use encryption to avoid detection and prosecution
    d. All of the above.

40. Identify the encryption system using private or secret key that must remain secret between the two parties.

    a. Running key cipher
    b. Asymmetric algorithm
    c. Symmetric algorithm
    d. Concealment cypher

41. What is the definition of DEA?

    a. Data encoding algorithm
    b. Data encoding application

    c.   Data encryption algorithm

    d.   Data encryption application

42. What is the definition of an algorithm's work factor?

    a.   The time it takes to encrypt and decrypt plaintext

    b.   The time it takes to break the encryption

    c.   The time it takes to implement arithmetic computation

    d.   The time it takes to apply substitution function

43. Identify the type of cipher classified as Caesar Cipher

    a.   Polyalphabetic substitution

    b.   Mono-alphabetic transposition

    c.   Mono-alphabetic substitution

    d.   Polyalphabetic transposition

44. Who was directly involved in the development of the first public key algorithm?

    a.   Adi Shamir

    b.   Broke Foot

    c.   Bruce Gram

    d.   Martin Hellman

45. Which attack executed against a cryptographic algorithm uses all possible keys until a key is discovered that can successfully decrypt the copytext?

    a.   Frequency analysis

    b.   Brute force

    c.   Ciphertext-only attack

    d.   Reverse engineering

46. Which of the following provides the preeminent definition of an encryption algorithm

a. Stream ciphers used for confidentiality
b. Detection of encryption mathematics
c. Mathematical functions used for encryption of an encryption algorithm
d. Detection of encryption authentication

47. What is the primary purpose of using one-way hashing on user password?

    a. It minimizes the amount of primary and secondary hacking
    b. It prevents cybercriminals from reading passwords in plaintext
    c. It avoids excessive processing of asymmetric algorithm
    d. It decreases replay attacks.

48. What is the meaning of DES?

    a. Data encryption system
    b. Data encryption standard
    c. Data encoding standard
    d. Data encoding signature

49. Identify the most secured encryption scheme

    a. Concealment cipher
    b. Symmetric algorithm
    c. Asymmetric algorithm
    d. One-time pad

50. Which of the following is an asymmetric algorithm?

    a. Two fish
    b. RC6
    c. RSA
    d. IDEA

51. Provide an accurate function of a TPM chip

    a. Responsible for supporting virtualization
    b. Responsible for public keys
    c. Responsible for hardware-based storage encryption key
    d. Enhances the CPU performance storage

52. If a cryptosystem is using a key size of 8 bits, what is the appropriate key space size?

    a. 32
    b. 64
    c. 256
    d. 78

53. What size of message digest does secure hash algorithm (SHA) produce?

    a. 128-bits
    b. 64-bits
    c. 160-bits
    a. 120-bits

54. As an organization IT Director, identify an acceptable technique to provide strong encryption service to users

    a. Using secrecy of the hash algorithm
    b. Using smaller key space to provide greater variety of strong key
    c. Using larger key space to provide greater variety of strong key
    a. Using hash function to provide greater variety of key space

55. Which one of the following items are true about RSA?

    a. Can be used for encryption and digital signature
    b. Can be used for key exchange

      c.   Developed at MIT by Ron Rivets, Adi Shamir and Leonard Adelman

      d.   All of the above

56. Which of the following item is the requirement for securing a Verna cypher?

      a.   Symmetric key must be encrypted with asymmetric key

      b.   Private key must be known only by the sender

      c.   The pad must be used just one

      d.   The existence of the key pad must be kept secret

57. What are the similarities between one-time pad and stream cipher?

      a.   Both are block cipher

      b.   Both use XOR for their encryption process

      c.   Both are vulnerable to leaner frequency cryptanalysis attacks

      d.   Both are symmetric algorithm processes

58. What is the major function of Diffie-Hellman algorithm?

      a.   Digital signature

      b.   Encryption

      c.   Key exchange

      d.   Hashing

59. Which algorithm did NIST choose to become the advanced encryption standard (AES) to replace (DES)?

      a.   Two-fish

      b.   IDEA

      c.   Randel

      d.   DEA

60. What size of hash value does MD2 generate?

    a. 156-bits
    b. 64-bits
    c. 128-bits
    d. 150-bits

61. Identify the standard used to describe PKI certificates.

    a. X.400
    b. X.509
    c. X.500
    d. X.50X

62. The ability to hide data and information within another data is known as

    a. Substitution
    b. Computation
    c. Steganography
    d. Hashing

63. The secret key used for data encryption one time only is known as

    a. Public key
    b. Key exchange
    c. Session key
    d. Mono-symmetric key

64. Knapsack is precisely what type of algorithm?

    a. Hashing
    b. Symmetric
    c. Asymmetric
    d. Encryption

65. Protocol used to implement secure channel between two devices in VPN operations is known as:

    a. TCP
    b. IPSec
    c. IPv4
    d. IPv6

66. The major component of IPSec must include two of the following:

    a. Integrity and user authentication
    b. Integrity and system authentication
    c. Confidentiality and authentication
    d. Trust and availability

67. Identify significant differences between symmetric and asymmetric algorithm

    a. Asymmetric algorithms are slower because they use substitution and transposition
    b. Symmetric algorithms are faster because they use substitution and transposition
    c. Asymmetric algorithms are vulnerable to cyber-attacks
    d. Asymmetric algorithms are easy to install and configure.

68. El Gamal is directly associated with which of the characteristics?

    a. A hash algorithm
    b. A symmetric algorithm
    c. A public key algorithm
    d. A message key algorithm

69. Which of the following best defines Certificate Authority?

    a. Organization that issues certification authority
    b. Organization that controls encryption authority
    c. Organization that validates certificate authority

    d.   Organization that controls key algorithm

70. Identify the best item used by IPSec management.

    a.   TCP/IP
    b.   IKE
    c.   MPLS
    d.   UDP

71. Cyber-attack that sends packets with same source and destination addresses is classified as

    a.   Synchronous attack
    b.   Data validation attack
    c.   Denial-of-service attack
    d.   Distribution attack

72. What key is used to create a digital signature?

    a.   The receiver's private key
    b.   The sender's private key
    c.   The receiver's public key
    d.   The sender's public key

73. When a sender cannot deny sending message to the receiver is referred as

    a.   Authenticity
    b.   Data integrity
    c.   Nonrepudiation
    d.   Data algorithm

74. Identify the type of protocol used commonly to authenticate official users on dial-up connection

    a.   PPTP
    b.   CHAP

c. IPSec
d. UDP

75. Which of the following is an example of pre-emptive physical access control?

    a. Implementation of reemployment background check
    b. Conducting employee's daily security training
    c. Configuring access control list on firewall
    d. Locking laptop ducking stations

76. Matthias Akuda requested stepwise process on how one-time password generating token can be viewed as a two-factor authentication mechanism.

    a. Matthias will have to authenticate with the system using his user name and one-time password, which is two-factor
    b. Matthias will have to authenticate to two systems using his user name and one-time password, which is two-factor
    c. Matthias will have to authenticate to a token device using his PIN prior to creating a one-time password. Matthias will have to create token device, authenticate his PIN
    d. during the system authentication process, which is a two-factor.

77. Matthias Akuda continues to press forward with fortitude to implement a strong authentication system, which of the following will best support his determination.?

    a. Smart reader card
    b. User name and password
    c. Biometric device
    d. Token card that requires a PIN

78. If a police officer locks a door so that a suspect cannot access to his (the suspect's) own computer without a warrant, what would be the most likely outcome?

    a. The evidence will be excluded because the officer seized it without a warrant.
    b. The evidence will be excluded because it does not meet the Daubert standard.
    c. The evidence will be admitted; this is not a warrantless seizure.
    d. The evidence will be admitted; the officer acted in good faith.

79. Identify the United States federal agency that is most responsible for cybercrime investigation outcome

    a. The FBI
    b. Homeland Security
    c. NSA
    d. Secret service

80. What type of encryption uses a different key to encrypt the message than it uses to decrypt the message?

    a. private key
    b. asymmetric
    c. symmetric
    d. secure key
    e. Top of Form

81. What does it mean to validate findings?

    a. To ensure they meet Daubert standards
    b. To ask a colleague if they agree with your findings
    c. To repeat the test
    d. To re-read your notes to see if you followed SOP

82. What part of a cloud implementation provides the virtual servers with access to resources?

    a. Hypervisor
    b. Resource monitor
    c. Resource auditor
    d. Virtual Manager

83. Where is the data for roaming phones stored?

    a. GSM
    b. BTS
    c. VLR
    d. HLR

84. A virus that changes as it spreads is known as

    a. Multipartite
    b. Polymorphic
    c. Armored
    d. Changeling

85. Which of the following best describes the relationship between COBIT and ITIL

    a. A COBIT is a model for IT governance, whereas ITIL is a model for corporate governance.
    b. A COBIT provides a corporate governance roadmap, whereas ITIL is a customizable framework for IT service management?
    c. A COBIT defines IT goals, whereas ITIL provides the process-level
    d. steps on how to achieve them. A COBIT provides a framework for achieving security goals, whereas ITIL defines a framework for achieving IT service-level goals.

86. Robert has been given the responsibility of installing doors that provide diverse types of protection. He has been told to install doors that provide fail-safe, fail-secure, and fail-soft protection. Which of the following statements is true about secure door types?

    a. Fail-soft defaults to the sensitivity of the area.
    b. Fail-safe defaults to locked.
    c. Fail-secure defaults to unlocked.
    d. Fail-secure defaults to double locked.

87. Layer 2 of the OSI model has two sublayers. What are those sublayers, and what are two IEEE standards that describe technologies at that layer?

    a. LCL and MAC; IEEE 802.2 and 802.3
    b. LCL and MAC; IEEE 802.1 and 802.3
    c. Network and MAC; IEEE 802.1 and 802.3
    d. LLC and MAC; IEE E 802.2 and 802.3

88. The NIST organization has defined best practices for creating continuity plans. Which of the following phases deals with identifying and prioritizing critical functions and systems?

    a. Identify preventive controls.
    b. Develop the continuity planning policy statement
    c. Develop recovery strategies
    d. Conduct the business impact analysis.

89. Cyber law categorizes computer-related crime into three categories. Which of the following is an example of a crime in which the use of a computer would be categorized as incidental?

    a. Carrying out a buffer overflow to take control of a system
    b. The electronic distribution of child pornography
    c. Attacking financial systems to steal funds
    d. Capturing passwords as they are sent to the authentication server

90. Which of the following describes the differences between the data encryption standard and the Rivets-Shamir Adelman algorithm?

    a. DES is symmetric, and RSA is asymmetric
    b. DES is asymmetric, and RSA is symmetric
    c. DES has hash function and RSA has algorithm
    d. DES can create a public and a private key and RSA creates one key

91. Which of the following best describes a certificate authority?

    a. An organization that issues private key and similar algorithm
    b. An organization that validates encryption processes
    c. An organization that verifies encryption keys
    d. An organization that issues certificates

92. Which PKI component contains a list of all the certifications that have been revoked?

    a. CA
    b. RA
    c. CRL
    d. OCSP

93. Identify the two main types of encryption algorithms

    a. Symmetric and Private Key
    b. Shared Key and Symmetric
    c. Asymmetric and Symmetric Key
    d. Private Key and Shared Key

94. Maurice and Felicia are life-time partners and they agreed to use an asymmetric cryptosystem to communicate with each other. Maurice is located at Udung-Esin, AFI-UDA and Felicia resides at Adadia, AFI-UDA, three miles from each other and have exchanged encryption keys by utilizing digital certificates signed

by a mutual certificate authority. If Maurice wanted to send Felicia an encryption message, what key must Maurice use to encrypt the message?

    a. Maurice's public key
    b. Maurice's private key
    c. Felicia's public key
    d. Felicia's private key

95. When Felicia receives the encrypted message from Maurice, what key must Felicia use to decrypt the message?

    a. Maurice's public key
    b. Maurice's private key
    c. Felicia's public key
    d. Felicia's private key

96. Which one of the following keys would Maurice not possess in the process?

    a. Felicia's public key
    b. Felicia's private key
    c. Maurice's public key
    d. Maurice's private key

97. In the entire process, Felicia will like to digitally sign the message that she sends to Maurice, what key must she use to create the digital signature?

    a. Felicia's public key
    b. Felicia's private key
    c. Maurice's public key
    d. Maurice's private key

98. Identify the principle and standard supporting the encryption algorithm to be open to public inspection

a. Security through anonymity
b. Intrusion prevention operation
c. Kirchhoff principle
d. Enigma machine

99. Name the person who help to develop the first public key algorithm

a. Kirchhoff
b. Martin Hellman
c. Enigma operation
d. Bruce Schneider

Answers Page: Chapter 5

1. C
2. A
3. B
4. B
5. C
6. C
7. C
8. B
9. B
10. B
11. A
12. C
13. A
14. B
15. B
16. B
17. B
18. B
19. D
20. B
21. A
22. C
23. C
24. A
25. C
26. B
27. A
28. A
29. B
30. B
31. D
32. B
33. D
34. A

35. D
36. B
37. C
38. A
39. B
40. B
41. C
42. B
43. C
44. D
45. C
46. C
47. B
48. B
49. B
50. D
51. C
52. C
53. C
54. C
55. A
56. C
57. B
58. C
59. C
60. C
61. B
62. C
63. C
64. C
65. B
66. B
67. B
68. C
69. A
70. B

71. C
72. C
73. C
74. B
75. D
76. C
77. C
78. A
79. D
80. B
81. C
82. D
83. C
84. D
85. C
86. A
87. D
88. D
89. B
90. A
91. D
92. A
93. C
94. C
95. D
96. B
97. B
98. C
99. B

Index

PAGE

References

Aquilina, James M., Casey, Eoghan & Malin, Cameron (2008). Malware Forensics: Investigation and Analyzing Malicious Code. Burlington, MA

Arthur, M. B. & Rousseau, D. M. (1996). (eds.), "The Boundary less Career: A New Employment Principle for a New Organizational Era," New York: Oxford University Press, http://findarticles. com/p/articles/mi_m4035/is_3_43/ai_53392863/.

Assenter M. & Tobey, D. (2011). "Enhancing the Cybersecurity Workforce," IT Professional, (13),1, pp. 12-15. Http://ieeexplore.ieee.org/xpl/ freeabs_all.jsp?arnumber=5708280.

Association of Chief Police Officer (ACOP) (2015), The Protocol on the Appropriate Handling of Crimes in Prison.

Barton, Chris, Bohme, Rainer, Clayton, Richard, van Eeten, Michel J.G., Levi, Michael, Tyler, Moore, and Savage, Stefan, (2012). "Measuring the Cost of Cyber Crime" (paper presented at the Weis 202 Workshop on the Economics of Information Security Berlin, Germany (June 25-26).

Bem, Derek, Feld, Francine, Ewa, Huebner, Ewa, & Bem, Oscar. (2008). Computer Forensic: Past, Present and Future: Journal of Information Science and Technology, University of Western Sydney, Australia.

Bennett, D (2011) "The Challenges Facing Computer Forensics Investigators in obtaining Information from Mobile Devices for Use in Criminal Investigations." http://articles.forensicfocus. com/2011/08/22/the-challenges-facing-computer-forensics-investigators-in-obtaining-information-from-mobile-devices-for-use-in-criminal-investigations.

Blair, Dennis, Huntsman Jr, Jon, Barrett, Craig, Gordon, Slade, Lynn III, William. J. Wince-Smith, Deborah, and Young, Michael K., (2014). "The IP Commission Report: The Report on the Commission of the Theft of American Intellectual Property." (Seattle, Washington, National Bureau of Asian Research: 2013), Last Accessed: 2/10/2014, http://www.ipcommission. Org/report/ IP_Commission_Report_052213.pdf.

Brown, Cameron S. D. (2015). Investigating and Prosecuting Cyber Crime: *Forensic Dependencies and Barriers to Justice.* Vol. 9 Issue 1 (55-119)

Bucci, Steven, Rosenzweig, Inserra (2014) "A Congressional Guide: Seven Steps to U.S. Security, Prosperity, and Freedom in Cyberspace." *Policy Analyst, Homeland Security and Cybersecurity.* Douglas and Sarah Allison Center for Foreign and National Security Policy.

Burton, Sharon L. & Bessette, Dustin (2015). War Against Identity Cyber Assault in a Social World. *The United States Cyber Security Magazine,* Volume 2, Number 1 (16-17).

Casey, Eoghan. (2000). *Digital Evidence and Computer Crime.* Second Edition. San Diego, CA: Academic Press.

Cashell, Brian, Jackson, William D., Jickling Mark and Webel Baird. (2014). "The Economic Impact of Cyber-Attacks," (Washington, D.C., Congressional Research Service: 2004), Last Accessed: 2/10/2014, http:// congressionalresearch.com/ RL32331/ document.php. DAKA Advisory, "Meeting the cyber security challenge in Indonesia: An analysis of threats and responses," (Jakarta, Indonesia, British Embassy in Indonesia, 2013), Last

Accessed: 2/10/2014, http://dakaadvisory. com/wpcontent/uploads/DAKA-Indonesia-cyber-security-2013-webversion.pdf. Financial Action Task Force, "Money Laundering & Terrorist Financing Vulnerabilities of Commercial Websites and Internet Payment Systems," (Paris, France Financial Action Taskforce OECD: 2008), Last Accessed: 2/10/2014, http://www.fatf-gafi. org/media/fatf/documents/reports/ML.

Castaldo, Chris (2015). "Why the Internet of Things, doesn't have to be a Security Nightmare." The United States Cyber Security Magazine, Volume 3, Number 7 (16-17).

Chapple, Mike and Seidi. (2016). Certified Information System Security Professional (CISSP) Official (ISC)2 Practice Tests. SYBEX-A Wilery Brand. Indianapolis, IN.

Cross, Michael. (2008). *Scene of the Cybercrime.* MA, Burlington, Syngress Publishing, Inc.

Dubai, UAE. (2008). Information Technology's role in providing high quality healthcare. Booz & Company. White Paper (2015) *Combating Cybercrime in the Healthcare Industry:* Cisco and affiliates.

Dye, Jessica, Axe, Joseph and Finkle, Jim. (2013). "Huge cyber bank theft spans 27 countries," Reuters, May 9, 2013, USA-crime-cyber crimeidUSBRE9480PZ20130509; "Six Arrested Over 45 Million Cyber Heist on Middle East Banks," Al Arabiya, November 19, 2013, http://english.alarabiya.net/en/business/banking-andfinance/2013/11/19/Six-arrested-over-45-million-cyber-heist-on-Middle-East-banks.html http://krebsonsecurity.com/2013/11/feds-charge-calif-brothers-in-cyberheists.

Eastton, Chuck and Taylor, Jeff Det. (2011). *Computer Crime, Investigation and the Law.* Boston: MA, Cengage Learning Course Technology.

Esin, Joseph O. (2017). *System Overview of Cyber-Technology in a Digitally Connected Society.* Author House. Bloomington, IN.

Esin, Joseph O. (2017). "Cybersecurity Professional Education and Inquiry." Washington Center for Cybersecurity Research and Development. https://www.washingtoncybercenter.com/publications-projects

Esin, Joseph O. (2016). Overview of Cyber Security: Endangerment of Cybercrime on Vulnerable Innocent Global Citizens. The International Journal of Engineering and Science (IJES) Volume 5, Issue 4, (2319-1805).

Farmer, Dan, Venema, Wietse. (2005). Forensic Discovery. Addison-Wesley Professionals.

Fitzgerald, Alvita and Schneider, Jessica. (2015). "Keep it Secret, Keep it Safe: Nine Steps to Maintaining Data Security." *The United States Cyber Security Magazine,* Volume 3, Number 7 (74-75).

Garrain, Dawn. (2017). *Computer Forensics Investigation Procedures and Response.* Course Technology, Boston, MA.

Givens, Austen D. (2015). "Strengthening Cyber Incident Response Capabilities through Education and Training in the Incident Command System" Journal of the National Cybersecurity Institute. Volume 2, Number 3 (65-75).

Grama, Joanna L. (2016) Excelsior *College CYS 541 Custom VitalBook, 2nd Edition.* Jones & Bartlett Learning. VitalBook file.

Harris, Shon (2008) ALL-IN-ONE Certified Information System Security Professional (CISSP) Examination Guide 4th Edition. Mc-Graw Hill. New York, N.Y.

Harris, Shon and Ham, Jonathan (2016). Certified Information System Security Professional (CISSP) Practice Exams. 4th Edition. Mc-Graw Hill. New York, N.Y.

Heintze, Hans-Joachim & Thielborger, Pierre (2016). From Cold War to Cyber War: Springer International Publishing, AG Switzerland.

Hoyte, B. (2012). "The need for Transnational and State-Sponsored Cyber Terrorism Laws and Code of Ethics" http://articles.forensicfocus.com/2012/09/28/the-need-for-transnational-and-state-sponsored-cyber-terrorism-laws-and-code-of-ethics.

Johnathan, Bridbord, (2013). CEOS Lead Digital Investigative Analyst Receives 2013 Federal Service Award from Office for Victims of Crime.

Johnson, Rob. (2011). *Security Policies and Implementation Issues, Jones & Bartlett Learning*, Burlington, MA.

Jones, Keith J, Bejtlich, Richard & Rose, Curtis W. (2006). *Real Digital Forensics: Computer Security and Incident Response.* Upper Saddle River, NJ: Pearson Education, Inc.

Kessler International - Forensic Accounting, Computer Forensics, Corporate Investigation. http://www.investigation.com/praccap/hightech/compforen.htm.

Kinyenje, Christine (2015). *Strategizing for Data Breach Risk Management. United States Cybersecurity Magazine* Vol. 3, NO. 8 (74-76).

Last, D. (2012). "Computer Analysts and Experts – Making the Most of GPS Evidence." http://articles.forensicfocus.com/2012/08/27/computer-analysts-and-experts-making-the-most-of-gps-evidence

LeClair, Jane and Ramsay, Sherri W. Ramsay (2015). *Protecting Our Future: Educating a Cybersecurity Workforce.* Hudson Whitman, Excelsior College Press. Albany: New York

LeClair, Jane and Ramsay, Keeley, Ashcroft (2015). *Protecting Our Future: Cybersecurity in our Digital Lives.* Hudson Whitman, Excelsior College Press. Albany: New York

LeClair, Jane and Ramsay, Rumsfeld, Donald (2013). *Protecting Our Future: Educating a Cybersecurity Workforce.* Hudson Whitman, Excelsior College Press. Albany: New York

LeClair, Jane A. (2016), "Understanding personal computers' hardware, operating systems and applications is in a good first step towards obtaining the knowledge and skill necessary for cyber literature." United States Cybersecurity Magazine, Vol 4, No. 10 (22-26).

LeClair, Jane & Keeley, Gregory (2015). *Protecting Our Future in Our Digital Lives*, Excelsior College Press. Albany, NY

Lewis, James A. and Baker, Stewart, (2014) "Estimating the Cost of fighting cybercrime. Accessed 2/10/2014, https://csis.org/event/ estimating-costcyber-crime-andcyber- espionage.

McClarkin, Emma (2014) "Cyber Crime- New Investigation Strategies and New Technologies," (Brussels, Belgium, Special Committee on Organized Crime, Corruption, and Money Laundering: 2012), Last accessed: 2/10/2014, http://www.europarl.europa. eu/meetdocs/2009_2014/documents/crim/dv/ mcclarkin_/ mcclarkin_en.pdf. Norton by Symantec, "2012 Norton Cyber Crime Report," (Mountain View, CA, Symantec: 2012), Last Accessed: 2/10/2014,http://nowstatic.norton.com/now/en/pu/ images/Promotions/2012/cyber crime Report/2012_Norton_ Cyber crime_Report_Master_FINAL_ 050912.pdf.

McMillan, Troy and Abernathy, Robin. (2014). *Certification Guide, Learn, Prepare and Practice for Examination Success CISSP.* Indianapolis, IN: University of Indiana Press.

Milazzo, C. (2012). "Searching Cell Phones Incident to Arrest: 2009 Update." http://www.policechiefmagazine.org/magazine/index. cfm?fuseaction=display&issueid=52009&category ID=3.

Muhlbaier, Lawrence H. (2003). *HIPAA Training Handbook for Researchers: HIPAA and Clinical Trials.* HcPro 1ˢᵗ Edition, Marblehead, MA.

Murphy, Sean P. (2015). *Healthcare Information Security and Privacy.* San Francisco, CA: McGraw Hill

NASW Center for Workforce Studies: National Association of Social Workers Washington, DC, http://workforce.socialworkers.org, March 2006.

National Institute of Standards and Technology (NIST). (2003). Test Results for Digital Data Acquisition Tool: FTK Imager 2.5.3.14. United States Department of Justice: Office of Justice Programs.

Nelson, Bill. (2004). *Guide to Computer Forensics and Investigations.* Boston, MA: Thomson Course Technology

Ngwang, Emmanuel N. (2016). Individual freedom, cyber security and the nuclear proliferation in a borderless land: Innovations and trade-offs in scientific progress. *The Journal of Educational Research and Technology (JERT)* 5 (5), pp. 17-38.

Perez, Evan & Diaz, Daniella. (2016). "White House announces retaliation against Russia: Sanctions, ejecting diplomats." *CNN Politics*

Reese, George. (2009). Cloud Application Architecture: Building Applications and Infrastructure in the Cloud. *O'Reilly Media.* Graven stein Highway North, Sebastopol: CA.

Shinder, Debra L. (2002). *Cybercrime: Computer Forensics Handbook.* Syngress Publishing, Inc. Rockland, MA:

Shinder, Debra Littlejohn & Tittel (Ed). (2002). *Scene of the Cybercrime Computer Forensics Handbook.* Rockland, MA.

Smith, John C. (2008). *History of the High Technology Crime Investigation Association* (HTCIA): Santa Clara (Silicon Valley) CA

Smith, Christen Marie. (2015). Building the Cyber force of the Future. *United States Cybersecurity Magazine*, Volume 3, Number 9 (43-55).

Stallings, Williams. (2015). *Cryptography and Network Security Principles and Practices.* Upper Saddle Valley, NJ: Prentice Hall.

Tohid, O. (2012). "Bin Laden bodyguard's satellite phone calls helped lead US forces to hiding place" http://www.csmonitor.com/World/ Asia-South-Central/2011/0502/Bin-Laden-bodyguard-s-satellite-phone-calls-helped-lead-US-forces-to-hiding-place.

Top U.S. Healthcare Story (2014): Cybersecurity, Forbes.

United Nation (2000). Tenth United Nations Congress on Prevention of Crime and Treatment Of Offenders. Vienna. www.un.org/press/ en/2000/20000410.soccp216.doc.html SOC/CP/216, 10 April 2000.

AUTHOR'S BACKGROUND

Professor Joseph O. Esin, chief publishing editor of *The Journal of Educational Research and Technology (JERT)*, holds a Bachelor's of Science in Biology from Saint Louis University, Saint Louis, Missouri; a Master's of Arts in Religious Studies, with emphasis on Moral Theology, from the Society of Jesus College of Divinity, Saint Louis, Missouri; and a Doctorate in Computer Education and Technology from the United States International University, San Diego, California. The State of California awarded him a Lifetime Collegiate Instructor's Credential in 1989, and in 1996, the United States Department of Justice approved and conferred on him the honor of "Outstanding Professor of Research" in recognition of his contributions to academic excellence.

He met the selection criteria for inclusion in the 1992–93, 1994–95, 1996–97 and 2015–2016 editions of *Who's Who in American Education* for demonstration of achievement and outstanding academic leadership in computer information technology, thereby contributing significantly to the betterment of contemporary society. Furthermore, he met the selection criteria for inclusion in the 1993–94 edition of the *Directory of International Biography*, Cambridge, England, for his distinguished professional service in information technology. From 1988 to 2000, he served as a professor of computer information technology, and from 1991 to 2000, a director of higher education accreditation operations, in accordance with the guidelines set forth by the Commission on Colleges. He was appointed an associate dean of academic affairs and a deputy provost at Paul Quinn College, Dallas, Texas, from 1997 to 2000. He is currently a professor of computer information systems at Jarvis Christian College (JCC), Hawkins, Texas, where his peers just elected him Vice President of JCC 2017-2018 Faculty Governance. In addition, he is a visiting professor of research at.

the University at Calabar, Nigeria; and a research associate at the Botanical Research Institute of Texas (BRIT).

Professor Esin has published several articles in professional journals among which are "High Level of Teachers' Apprehension (HLTA): About the Use of Computers in the Educational Process" in the *Journal of Educational Media & Library Science* (*JEMLS*) in 1991; "Computer Literacy for Teachers: The Role of Computer Technology in the Educational Process," also in *JEMLS* (1992); "Faculty Development: Effective Use of Applications Software in the Classroom for Instruction" (*JEMLS*, 1993); "Strategies for Developing and Implementing Academic Computing in Colleges and Universities" (*JEMLS*, 1994); "Strategic Planning for Computer Integration in Higher Education through the Year 2000" (*JEMLS*, 1994); "The Challenge of Networking Technologies" (*JEMLS*, 1995); and "The Design and Use of Instructional Technology in Schools, Colleges and Universities" (*JEMLS*, 1997). He also published "Decay of the Nigerian Education System," in the *Journal of Educational Research and Technology* (*JERT*) in 2013; "The Emerging Impact of Information Technology on Education and the Community" (*JERT*, 2013); "Balanced Salary Structure for Academic Professors and Allied Educators as a Pathway to Quality Education" (*JERT*, 2014); and "The Discovery of Computer Information Technology as an Avenue for Educational Transformation in a Changing Society of Today and Tomorrow" in *International Organization of Scientific Research Journal of Engineering* (*IOSR-JEN*) in 2014. In 2016, he published "Overview of Cyber Security: Endangerment of Cybercrime on Vulnerable Innocent Global Citizens" in *The International Journal of Engineering and Science (IJES-2016)* and "Analog to Digital: Overcoming Widespread Implementation of Wireless Information Technology on a Vulnerable Global Society" (*JERT,2016*), Cybersecurity Professional Education and Inquiry (2017) in the *Washington Center for Cybersecurity Research and Development* (*WCCRD*-2017), Imminent Cybersecurity Threats and Vulnerability of Organizations and Educational Systems (*WCCRD*-2017), Escalating Outcome of Cyber-Attacks on Healthcare Organizations (WCCRD-2017) and Escalating Outcome of Cyber-Attacks on Healthcare Organizations (WCCRD-2017).

He served as a member of Doctoral Dissertation Committees at Southern Methodist University, Dallas, Texas (1998–2000); Jackson State

University, Jackson, Mississippi (2010–2011); and University of Calabar, Nigeria (2014–2015). He is the author of *The Power of Endurance* (2008), *The Evolution of Instructional Technology* (2011), *The Messianic View of the Kingdom of God* (2011), *Global Education Reform* (2013) and *System Overview of Cyber-Technology in a Digitally Connected Global Society* (2017). Professor Esin's current research emphasis is on the *Landscape of Cybersecurity Threats and Forensic Inquiry.*

**He is guided by the philosophy that
"To achieve what is possible, you must attempt the impossible."**

Printed in the United States
By Bookmasters